PREACHING

JUDGES

Preaching Classic Texts

Preaching Apocalyptic Texts
Larry Paul Jones and Jerry L. Sumney

Preaching 1 Corinthians 13
Susan K. Hedahl and Richard P. Carlson

Preaching Genesis 12–36
A. Carter Shelley

Preaching Job
John C. Holbert

Preaching Luke-Acts
Ronald J. Allen

Preaching Resurrection
O. Wesley Allen, Jr.

Preaching Judges
Joseph R. Jeter, Jr.

PREACHING

JUDGES

JOSEPH R.
JETER, JR.

CHALICE
PRESS
ST. LOUIS, MISSOURI

Cover art: Stained-glass window "Deborah" by Marc Chagall, St. Stephens, Mainz,
  Germany. Photograph © The Crosiers.
Cover design: Mike Foley/Elizabeth Wright
Interior design: Wynn Younker/Hui-Chu Wang
Art direction: Michael Domínguez/Elizabeth Wright

This book is printed on acid-free, recycled paper.

Visit Chalice Press on the World Wide Web at
www.chalicepress.com

10 9 8 7 6 5 4 3 2 1   03 04 05 06 07 08

Library of Congress Cataloging–in–Publication Data

Jeter, Joseph R.
  Preaching Judges / Joseph R. Jeter, Jr.
  p. cm. – (Preaching classic texts)
  Includes bibliographical references and index.
  ISBN 0-8272-2977-1 (alk. paper)
  1. Bible. O.T. Judges–Sermons. I. Title. II. Series.
  BS1305.54.J48 2003
  222'.3206–dc22   2003014418

Printed in the United States of America

CONTENTS

For Brenda

Writing has been described as a lonely process. I understand that. But since this preface is being written at the end rather than the beginning of my journey with Judges, I can see from here how blessed I have been by the people who helped me along the way and made the journey more rewarding and less lonely. I am grateful to my colleague Toni Craven for discussions on the book of Judges and for sharing podiums with me as we attempted to make sense of it. Many of the ideas I have developed in this book I first heard from her. Scholar friends J. Cheryl Exum and Jon L. Berquist graciously read the entire manuscript. They not only offered creative approaches that found their way into the book but also saved me from many minor infelicities and major stupidities. I owe them my deepest thanks. I also wish to thank Lisa Davison and Valerie Pettys for their comments on sections of the book and J. Clinton McCann for sharing with me his commentary on Judges in the Interpretation series before it was published.

This book is dedicated to a person who is much more important to the world than I am. Brenda Sargent Jeter has been my beloved wife for over a quarter-century, the mother of our son, and one who has always been supportive of my work. But she has also labored for a generation on the front lines of public education as a school administrator, often spending her time dealing with angry people and mediating conflict, while I enjoyed the comfortable environs of higher education. We have expected our public schools not only to educate our children but also to solve the most difficult of our social problems, while under-funding, under-supporting, and under-thanking those who give unstintingly of themselves and for whom a forty-hour week would seem like a vacation. One other bond we share: school administrators and preachers are almost always portrayed as idiots in teen-oriented motion pictures. We smile and work on. And we would both do it again. How grateful I am for her wisdom, her goodness, and the pleasure of her company.

Introduction

If you are reading this, my first battle has been won. Persuading one to open the cover of a book entitled *Preaching Judges* is not an easy task. You have apparently done so on your own, for which I am grateful. Since we are both here, let me tell you why I have written this book and why I think you ought to read it. My love-hate affair with the book of Judges goes back some thirty years. In my Introduction to Hebrew Bible course in seminary, I was sick the day texts were chosen for intensive exegesis. When I returned to class, the only text left was the story of Jephthah and his daughter in Judges 11:34–40. I wrote that exegesis paper, but it took years to move from text to sermon. That sermon, updated, is found in this volume.

I also moved to other stories in Judges, studying them and wondering if they had a word for us today. The more time I spent with Judges, the more I came to appreciate this quirky, sometimes horrible book. When I began to think about writing a book for preachers about what and how to preach from Judges, the first questions I had to struggle with were: why would anyone want to preach from Judges, and more importantly, why would anyone want to hear a Judges-based sermon? In D. T. Niles's famous saying, preaching is described as "one beggar telling another beggar where to find bread."[1] Well, the only bread in Judges is found in a dream (7:13), denied to hungry people (8:5), and shared by men while a young woman is handed over to an abuser (19:5), then raped and murdered (19:29). Want a bite? A Judges-based sermon must find its meaning elsewhere. My preliminary sevenfold answer to the question "why preach from Judges?" is in the first chapter.

Before the series of which this book is a part was conceived, I thought to call my book about preaching from Judges *God Bless the Worst Book in the Bible*. Maybe that would make people open the cover, if only to see which book I had in mind. I also conceived this volume as the balancing bookend for the earlier book I edited with Cornish Rogers, *Preaching through the Apocalypse: Sermons from Revelation*. That book dealt with preaching from the most unusual book in the New Testament. This one considers what may well be the most unusual book in the Hebrew Bible. The differences are that this book is shaped to fit this series, and all the sermons and vignettes herein are mine. I have learned not to ask commentary writers for sermons. I cannot write commentaries, and most commentary writers cannot preach. Further, there are precious few contemporary commentaries on Judges. Were it not for feminist scholars, I suspect that Judges would be all but ignored today. I have read scores of scholarly works on Judges and learned from every one of them, but I have also kept in mind the preacher's difficult office, to stand and deliver on a weekly basis a significant, helpful word.

There are times when biblical scholarship and preaching seem to live in different worlds. For example, consider this statement by scholar Meir Sternberg:

> They [different scholars] speak as if there were one Bible for the historian, another for the theologian, another for the linguist, another for the geneticist, another for the literary critic. But there are not enough Bibles to go around, and even Solomon's wisdom cannot divide the only one we possess among the various claimants.[2]

A preacher looking at Sternberg's list of claimants might well agree with Sternberg that there is only one Bible for all but also ask if the people of God might be included in the list.

Historian of preaching Ronald E. Osborn had a vivid description of how this works, using a thalassic metaphor:

> On the surface of the sea the waves roll, the shifting winds drive the spray now in one direction, now in

another, and occasionally a storm blows out its fury....
In our analogy the waves may be taken to represent
the theologians and professors, constantly in movement,
frequently intriguing, sometimes dazzling; the winds
and occasional storms are the contemporary schools
and trends, the controversies of the day which now and
then manifest their fury, but soon are spent.

Beneath the surface move the currents and cross-
currents, mighty rivers of cold or warmth, like our Gulf
Stream, sweeping imperiously across thousands of
miles, changing the climates of continents, determining
the course of the world's shipping and of history. The
currents represent the major movements of Christian
theology which affect the life of the churches and the
preaching of the gospel for generations or a century.

Below these moving streams which so readily alter
conditions on the surface rests the great deep. Cold
and dark it lies, heaving with the pulsation of its own
movement, but untroubled by the waves or surface
storms and relatively undisturbed by the currents,
though in some ways affected by them. The
oceanographer may correct our description of the
unfathomed depths, but they may be taken to represent
the faith of the people, the possession of the wise and
the foolish, expressing itself in life and work and
worship, all but unaware of the thinking of the
theologians.[3]

The three "strata" of the ocean may be designated the
surface, the currents, the deep—academic theology, major
movements of Christian thought, the faith of the people.[4]
Preachers, then, while familiar with the crashing waves and
the strong currents, still have to fish the depths, still have to
preach in ways that will reach people at their profoundest levels
of concern and experience.

Here is an example of the problem. Writing about structural
criticism, a noted biblical scholar looked at the three passages
in Judges where judge-deliverers hold the "fords of the Jordan"

against enemies. He then said, "To use the language of Levi-Strauss, the middle passage mediates the opposition between the other two."[5] Well, the middle passage may be a mediator in Levi-Strauss's language, but not in the language of history. The *Middle Passage,* perhaps the primary metaphor in African-American experience, does not mediate, but explodes the relationship between Africa and the Americas.

Thinking about structures instead of slavery when speaking of the middle passage is for many people like hearing the "William Tell Overture" without thinking of the Lone Ranger. When scholars ignore the language of the people, the people ignore scholars.[6] Preachers are often caught in the middle, standing with one foot in the academy and the other in the church, one in reason and the other in faith, and it is often hard for them to keep their balance. In my attempt to do just that, I have subjected unsuspecting congregations and conferences to sermons based on some of the most horrible literature ever written, in a continuing honest quest for words, pictures, and ideas from these texts that can make a difference in how we live.

I hope this book will provide a useful resource for preachers seeking to deal homiletically with these old texts and with some of today's most difficult problems. The first chapter introduces the book and my approach to it. After that, we engage the major stories and themes of Judges story by story. In each chapter, I offer a few opening comments about the story itself, and then offer sermons and other homiletical moves to demonstrate my approach to the stories. Five complete sermons are included: on Deborah, Gideon, Jephthah's daughter, Samson, and the wife of the Levite.[7] Also included are homiletical moves, or vignettes, or what Ian Macpherson would call kindling, or Halford Luccock would call diversions, for the stories of Adonibezek, Achsah, Othniel, Ehud, Abimelech, the minor judges, Micah and the Danites, and others.[8] Perhaps these may inspire metaphors for current events that need to be addressed, while providing enough distance to make them bearable. They might also be useful to preachers seeking to ground contemporary problems in a biblical landscape, helping people to see, if nothing else, that we are not the first ever to face these problems.

When we are dealing with texts as troubling–and sometimes as horrific–as those we find in Judges, it can be difficult to preach from these texts in the traditional way: here is what it says; here is what it means. For example: in Exodus, God delivers the Ten Commandments, including number six: "Thou shalt not kill" (KJV). But in Judges God is directly responsible for the deaths of hundreds of thousands of people. For this and other reasons, the picture of God in Judges is not very pretty. Homiletician Paul Scott Wilson has written that preachers should "ask of every biblical text, 'What is God doing in or behind the events of this passage?'"[9] For some texts in Judges the apparent answer is "killing people." This can drive us toward both anger and confusion. We shall have to dig deeper and reach further for understanding.

Thus, in dealing with texts such as many in Judges, we sometimes have to take oblique approaches to the material. This might include using five newer interpretative approaches:

1. *Intertextuality*: reading the Judges text with or through another text. The sermon on Jephthah's daughter makes use of this method.[10]

2. *Deconstruction*: reading between the lines and along the margins of the text, looking not only for what it says that has been ignored, but also for what it does not say. I have borrowed, for example, Danna Fewell's deconstruction of 1:11 for my piece on the City of Books.[11] I am also aware that deconstruction is a very complex phenomenon and that I am using strategies associated with deconstruction and not deconstruction itself. Scholars are not agreed on the definition or meaning of the term.

3. *Virtual history*: reading the text by asking "what if" the story had happened in a different way.[12] My sermon on Gideon uses this approach.

4. *Subaltern reading*: "history from below." This is a post-colonial attempt to achieve a nonelitist reading of history.[13] It

writes history from the people's perspective, not from that of the lords and rulers of the land. My pieces about Jael and Sisera's mother make some use of this approach, as do others in this book. New approaches to biblical study based on archaeology have gone so far as to suggest that the Hebrews were highland folk who rebelled against their lowland oppressors and established a religious society.[14] This being the case, one could claim that the whole Hebrew Bible is a subaltern reading.

5. *Re-telling the Story*: Similar to some of the others, this approach refers to a process whereby, without violating the integrity of the text, we try to read it in a different way, reshaping the sermon to work creatively with the retold text. This is the method I tried to follow in the sermon on the Levite's wife. As E. K. Brown says, "There is nothing magical in reading. It is in re-reading that some magic may lie."[15] And Thomas Troeger is even more bold when he speaks of the "infinite translatability" of the biblical stories.[16]

By the way, I was sternly warned against all of these when I was in school. Most of us have been surprised to find that the illegitimate tools we used under cover of night to get at meanings for our people, hoping our professors would not find out, now are generally accepted and have, in fact, scholarly names. In working with these approaches, we have to remember, in Fewell's words, "This does *not* mean that a text can say anything that a reader wants it to say. Texts have rights, too. Texts have constraints."[17] We do have a responsibility to the text, but we also have a responsibility to our people. If they cannot process the text in its raw form, or if they cannot hear the gospel through a traditional sermon, we may need to reread or recraft or both. In this book, for example, you will find sermon as comparison of texts, deconstructed and retold story, virtual and subaltern history. You will also find sermon as drama, poetry, and as written, not oral, instrument.

Another rule for writers that I violate herein, with apologies to poor Adonibezek, is that one should not mention current events in a book. To do so, the claim goes, is to date the book and thus shorten both its shelf life and its usefulness. But I cannot follow that advice precisely because this is a book about preaching and sermons (with their Bible-and-newspaper character) that exist in the mode of immediacy: for these people in this time and place.[18] As I write, I mention from time to time events of the day that could be engaged by the text at hand.

This book was completed prior to the events of September 11, 2001. But the horror of that day forced me to reopen my manuscript in several places, including a new piece on Samson as terrorist. Maybe my long relationship with Judges has left me biased, but I believe that it was for times such as these that these fascinating old stories were preserved.

CHAPTER 1

Why Preach from Judges?

The book of Judges forms the pivot of what has been called the Deuteronomistic History, connecting the Moses-Joshua stories of Deuteronomy and Joshua with the David-Solomon stories of Samuel and Kings. The theory of a Deuteronomistic History as an appropriate description of Joshua through 2 Kings was first propounded by Martin Noth in 1943.[1] This theory is now under attack (or, more gently, critique) in various ways from various perspectives. Was there a Deuteronomistic school or not? Was the work of the so-called Deuteronomistic historian(s) preexilic, exilic, or postexilic? Can these stories actually be called historical? Is Judges pro-monarchical or anti-monarchical? All these questions are currently in play. And there appear to be no easy answers. What we can say is that at the beginning of this "history" the Israelites won a land; at the end they lost it. At the beginning they had charismatic leaders, flawed though they may have been; at the end they had a failed monarchy.

At the middle of this story, at the pivot, we find the book of Judges. This book speaks of some two hundred years (more or less)[2] in the life of Israel and was written hundreds of years after the "fact." If fact and legend are blurred in these stories, it should not be a surprise to us. One approach then is to say that Judges represents the remembered stories of a period in Israel's past, a period of failed conquest, of social, political, and religious disintegration. Such remembered stories are critical to a nation's soul and character. For example, Americans who remember with pride the nation's "manifest destiny" and forget the travesties perpetrated on native Americans, who remember the glories of wars and forget the stories of slavery and racism, beget a skewed memory and may find themselves repeating some of our most regrettable national errors.

Who and what were the judges who give the book its name? North Americans tend to imagine a black-gowned severe-looking person sitting behind a bench high above a courtroom. The word *judge,* which has a juridical meaning in English, has a broader meaning in Hebrew. The juridical factor is present, for we read that Deborah sat under a palm tree in Ephraim and "the Israelites came up to her for judgment" (4:5). But *shophet* can also mean "ruler" or "military leader."[3] And there is a third factor, for the authority of the judges involved "the spirit of Yahweh" coming upon them. So we are talking about people who variously possessed judicial, military, and spiritual authority and power. Combine Joan of Arc with Judge Roy Bean, the law west of the Pecos, and you have a close approximation to these unusual people.

Twelve judges are in the book, six we call major (Othniel, Ehud, Deborah, Gideon, Jephthah, Samson), and six we call minor (Shamgar, Tola, Jair, Ibzan, Elon, Abzon). Their stories tell of military and moral success and failure and of the bumpy relationship these people had with the Spirit of God. Perhaps the major problem for us is that the remembered stories of these judges and other characters in the book include some of the most horrific literature ever written, stories that Phyllis Trible has called "texts of terror."[4]

This leads to the most critical question addressed by this book. Why preach from Judges? After all, the original title of Trible's book was *Texts of Terror:* Unpreached *Stories of Faith.*[5] Other important scholars believe we should continue to refrain from preaching these stories. Elisabeth Schüssler Fiorenza suggested:

> Christian *teaching* must preserve all traditions, precisely to preserve the multiformity of the written canon. Christian *preaching,* however, must discern between oppressive texts and liberating ones: only the latter deserve a place in proclamation.[6]

And Barnabas Lindars said:

Judges is a remembered as a book of heroes. That may well have value for a warlike people, to encourage them to fight. But we may well ask what religious value it has. Should it perhaps be banned from liturgical use, on the grounds that it does nothing to promote faith and Christian living?[7]

These are strong arguments. What do the chopping off of thumbs and toes, bathroom humor, driving tent pegs through heads, sacrificing daughters, dumb jokes, locker room sex stories, rape, and dismemberment have to do with the gospel, much less preaching? That is not an easy question, for these and many more offensive stories are found in Judges. I begin my answer with the following seven affirmations.

1. "In Praise of What Persists"[8]

I accept the idea of the canon and its value and authority, not so much for its perfection as for its persistence.[9] There is an essay by George Dennison in which he reflects on those great works, people, and events that have shaped his life. Books and paintings, teachers, protest marches–solitary and corporate experiences–did not "happen" and disappear. Somehow they "made a shock in the soul" that jolted him from his trajectory and changed his life. In honor and appreciation, Dennison calls his essay "In Praise of What Persists." So what persists in the religious life of a people? Many things, of course, but most vividly their trust, conscious and unconscious, in the Bible.

I grew up under the influence of a nineteenth-century preacher named Alexander Procter, one of those classical liberals who said, "I never believe anything just because it's in a book."[10] So I do not call the scriptures sacred. Theologian John Cobb taught me that only God is sacred. On the other hand, I have an abiding love for and trust in the Bible. Not only because homiletical sparks may sometimes fly when I go to a text but also because of the sheer persistence of scripture. No book has been so misused and abused; no book has been so hammered or ignored. And yet, like the roly-poly bug, it bounces back upright, always ready for new encounters.

In the year 1620, when the Pilgrim fathers and mothers were leaving from England and Holland for America, pastor John Robinson was asked on what basis they would build their colony in the new world. "We believe," said Robinson, "that there is yet more light to break forth from the Word of God."[11] Was it because they were such wonderful people? Was it because they had the correct theology and no one else did? Was it because they were God's specially chosen people? No. It was because they believed with all their hearts that the meaning of the Bible had not yet been exhausted, that there was more truth there about God than had yet been discovered, more light to break forth from the sacred pages of God's Word. Robinson spoke the truth. The most magical moments of my life have come at the feet of preachers who climbed into the text and then came back with new ideas in their head, passion in their hearts, and burning coals or cool breezes on their lips.

I have a lecture on videotape by Fred Craddock that I show to my classes. It is twenty years old now and still the best I have ever seen and heard on the subject of preaching. My students love it. I have seen it about fifty times now, and although Craddock is the best there is at our craft, the lecture begins to wear thin. Over the years I have become aware of those moments where he overstates his case, is unsure of how to proceed, uses images that do not quite work, and so on. The shelf life of the lecture has expired for me, as does that of all our works and sermons. But I have never gone to scripture and come away empty-handed. Of course, what I find there is often *not* what I am looking for, but it is persistently there. My preaching ministry will eventually falter and stop because of poor health or a failure of imagination, but it will not come to a standstill because its source in scripture has run dry. And this is true far before and beyond my little ministry. Scripture has not run dry in the past. It will not run dry in the future.

The authority of scripture poses another difficult question, one in which each of us has to carve out a position somewhere between the calcified literalism of those who aver that "God said it, I believe it, and that settles it," and the laissez-faire approach of the scholars who said recently, "What we like is canon; what we don't like isn't," and "Who cares what Paul thought?"

Another scholar said to me that we have to get over the idea that the Bible is authoritative for our lives. I understand from whence he speaks. He has spent his entire life handling the texts of the Hebrew Bible, turning them over and over in his hands, dealing with the creepy-crawlies that live just under the texts like bugs under a rock. Finally the texts have lost not only their authority for him but also their savor.

Perhaps the best response to his position takes its cue from Arthur John Gossip's classic sermon preached after the sudden and unexpected death of his wife:

> I do not understand this life of ours. But still less can I comprehend how people in trouble and loss can fling away peevishly from the Christian faith. In God's name, fling to what? Have we not lost enough without losing that too?[12]

Similarly, if the Bible is not authoritative for us, what is? Are we not then reduced to the other three shaky legs of the famous quadrilateral: tradition, reason, and experience? And the book of Judges should give us ample warning about placing all our trust in any of these. The Hebrews came to the end of Judges with everyone doing "what was right in their own eyes" (21:25). And it was a disaster.

The first reason for reading, teaching, and preaching from Judges is the mountaineer's rationale: because it is there, persistently there. The second reason is that we believe it to be important. We work with scripture because we believe God's word lingers therein or close by. And we offer our praise and thanksgiving for the persistent nature of that presence.

2. "Awaiting More Light"

Having said that I accept the idea of the canon, let me hasten to add that I do not accept the idea of plenary inspiration or literal interpretation. To say, as a recent writer of a letter to my local newspaper did, that God spoke every word of the Bible is to have a very low theology indeed. Reading the words and deeds attributed to God in Judges quickly disabuses one of such a biblical theology. The Bible is inescapably culturally conditioned. People thousands of years ago may have believed that God ordained the slaughter of thousands and the sacrifice of daughters, that the odor of animals sacrificed as burnt offerings was pleasing to the olfactory glands of God, but I do not.

To use a non-Judges example, I have never preached from Genesis 22. I simply cannot. Perhaps someday I will find a way to preach the Abraham-Isaac story, but that time is not yet. Like Abraham, I have an only son, and if God were to tell me to take my son up a mountain and sacrifice him there, then God and I would be quite finished with each other. The fact that there is a ram in the thicket matters not to me. It is already too late. God fails miserably in this story.[13] And so the only way I can even imagine to preach from this text would be to preach against it. Homiletician Ronald J. Allen reminds us that at times we must preach the gospel against certain texts that fly in the face of that good news.[14] Judges gives us plenty of such texts. So while I do not take the stories in Judges as the *ipsissima verba* (the exact words) of God, I do take them seriously as canon, as the record of a people's struggle and often failure to understand what it means to be in covenant with God. Sometimes I preach under their guidance. Sometimes I have to preach against them. Sometimes I place them in that drawer of my desk I have labeled "awaiting more light." Phyllis Trible, writing about Genesis 22, gives me hope for my work with some all but impossible texts from Judges when she says, brilliantly: "Take your interpretation of this story, your only interpretation, the one which you love, and sacrifice it on the mount of hermeneutics."[15] I have spent a lot of time walking around that mount, looking up, trying to get a better view. Every once in a while the clouds break, and I believe that what I see is worth sharing.

3. "In-between Times: Then and Now"

Judges tells the story of an in-between time in the political and religious life of the Hebrew people in the land of Canaan, between the "conquest" and the monarchy, a time that was probably more good than bad. But since the general trend, both politically and religiously, was downward, what were remembered and retold were not the stories of the good and peaceful times, but the stories of various crisis times. In-between times are often seen as dull and uninteresting. The truth is that they are fascinating. The decay of systems and the seeds of the future are available for inspection. What is not available is any agreed-on interpretation of the time. We live in such an in-between time today, between modernity and whatever it is that the future will be called. Empires are collapsing; power is shifting; economies are changing; religious sensibilities are in flux. As strange as it sounds, to read Judges is to look in a mirror, to see in many ways a proto-portrait of our own time. Some of the themes that appear and reappear in Judges are profoundly current, such as terrorism, political morality, family relationships (especially father-daughter relationships), and generational differences. Perhaps the two most prominent and timely issues are leadership—religious and political—and violence.[16] Karl Barth's famous dictum that we should preach with a newspaper in one hand and a Bible in the other certainly lends itself to occasions when the newspaper screams of trouble and the Bible is open to Judges.[17]

Judges is crisis literature, and more and more often preachers and congregations find themselves in crisis on Sunday mornings: public, congregational, or personal crisis. Many preachers seek to avoid or ignore crises in their sermons, preaching a "feel-good" gospel when their people feel bad. In my work with crisis preaching, I suggest that to be honest with and helpful to people, we have to begin by "speaking the truth that is in the room."[18] Judges often allows us to stand our crisis up next to a biblical crisis for help in understanding whether the way we are going will most likely lead to resolution or disaster.

Another way of saying this is to ask: can sad or tragic circumstances best be addressed by happy texts only? Certainly not always. At the center of the Christian faith stands a cross. Imagine that Jesus had lived a long and happy life and died rich and full of years. Would Christianity be the same? Would it even exist? No, and perhaps not. But his suffering has touched a responsive chord in suffering people down through the centuries. Among the things we have learned from Jesus is that we often minister to one other through our own pain. To use Henri Nouwen's phrase, Jesus is and we can become "wounded healers."[19] Similarly, I believe that "wounded" texts such as those in Judges can help bring healing through the sharing of their own agony, through the telling of their own sad stories. Nouwen wrote that "the main task of the minister is to prevent people from suffering for the wrong reasons."[20] One can hardly describe Judges better than that—people suffering for the wrong reasons: disloyalty, idolatry, rash vows, bad worship, bad ministry, a misguided sense of honor, and so forth. With these lessons to guide us, can we do better?

4. "Who Are We, That God Is Mindful of Us?"

Judges provides an antidote to the enduring belief that people in the Bible were so much better than we are that the Bible's lessons cannot be useful to us. Many believe that biblical lessons are designed for those who live on a much higher plane. To the contrary, Judges shows us people who were certainly no better than we and probably a whole lot worse. Even more amazing, and encouraging is that God was able to use some of these people for God's purposes, however suspicious of those purposes we may be. Hearing that, many of us may come to believe, perhaps for the first time, that we can figure in God's plans.

5. "Listen to the Muffled Voices"

Although most of the stories in Judges are set in the male-dominated biblical world of war and politics, more women are present in these stories than in almost any other book in the Bible. While there are comparatively fewer contemporary studies of Judges than of most other books, some of the very finest feminist biblical scholars have been drawn to Judges. As a result we have some excellent studies of gender in the Bible that allow us to read between the lines of these texts and find useful lessons for gender issues in our time.

Thomas Troeger has an interesting perspective on this. Writing about how one can flip from one news program to another on television and see almost the same thing and the same people, he reminds us:

> Before preachers become haughty about the media, we need to examine how we use the Bible. It is easy for sermons to become like the media's cameras, always focusing on the same characters, and not giving adequate play to those voices that have been buried by our constant attention to the chief players. One of the most significant gifts to preaching from liberation and feminist theologies has been the way they have helped us recover the muffled voices that are in the Bible and in our world. This act of recovery often breaks open texts so that the light of God streams from the familiar story with dazzling brightness. [21]

A good example of this is found in the well-known aphorism of Harry Emerson Fosdick, who reminded preachers in 1928 that "people don't come to church because they're dying to find out about the Jebusites."[22] All these years later, this line still seldom fails to get a laugh. And yet, who do we find at a key point in Judges? That's right, the Jebusites. In chapter 19, the Levite and his wife are journeying toward his home in Ephraim when night comes. They have arrived at Jerusalem, but pass it by because it is the "city of the Jebusites…this city of foreigners" (19:11–12). So they press on to Gibeah, a Benjaminite town, and stay there. That night the wife is raped and murdered by townsmen. We are left to realize they would no doubt have been better off with foreigners than kinsmen, with Jebusites rather than their own people. Nobody wants to know about the Jebusites, but maybe somebody should learn.

6. "What Hath God Wrought?"

The most important and difficult theological issue in Judges is the question of God. Perhaps the central tenet of our faith is that God is good. Unfortunately this affirmation has drowned in a sea of syrupy rhymes and feelings. As a result, it is largely unexamined today. What does it mean to say that God is good? One approach to this question is through a kind of deconstruction, increasing our understanding of a positive affirmation by examining its negative. And as I said in the Introduction, in many places in Judges, God is *not* good.[23]

Sitting and suffering in our churches are large numbers of people who are angry at God, who wonder why God "did" some thing to them or someone they love and who are at a loss to deal with these feelings of anger and frustration. They believe that the very idea of being angry with God is sacrilegious and sinful. And so they sit and suffer in silence. Seeing other people, biblical people, struggling with what sometimes appears to be a cruel and hostile God, can open new avenues of dealing with that pain or at least assuage our loneliness. We are not the first ones who ever felt this way. Hearing how people failed God and how God failed them in the early struggles of people to relate to God can create a landscape in which our own struggles can be better engaged. As biblical scholar Walter Harrelson frequently reminds those who will listen, it is better to take out our anger on God than on one another.

In a season finale of the award-winning television series *The West Wing* on May 16, 2001, President Bartlet's beloved administrative assistant is killed by a drunk driver. After the funeral service in the National Cathedral, the President orders the cathedral sealed. He is left alone and begins walking toward the chancel, looking up, saying as he goes:

> There's a tropical storm that's gaining speed and power. They say we haven't had a storm this bad since you took out that tender ship of mine in the North Atlantic last year. 68 crew. You know what a tender ship does? It fixes the other ships. It doesn't even carry guns. It just goes around and fixes the other ships and delivers the mail. That's all it can do. *Gratias tibi ago, domine....*
>
> Yes, I lied, it was a sin, I've committed many sins, have I displeased you, you feckless thug? 3.8 million new jobs, that wasn't good? Increased foreign trade, bailed out Mexico, 30 million new acres of land for conservation, put Mendoza on the bench, we're not fighting a war, and I raised three children, that doesn't buy me out of the doghouse? *Haec credam a deo pio, a deo iusto, a deo scito? Cruciatus in crucem. Tuus in terra*

servus, nuntius fui. Officium perfeci. Cruciatus in crucem. Eas in crucem.[24]

Yes, that was television. But many people have actually felt that way, lacking either the courage or the words to tell God about it. As the old rabbinic saying goes, "If you cannot pray, then curse God. That way at least you're in relationship." Struggling with God is a type of spiritual discipline that can bring us closer to God. And that struggle is vividly pictured in the book of Judges.

7. "We Want a Story!"

The motion picture called *The Wonderful World of the Brothers Grimm* tells the story of two brothers. One was a successful scholar and historian, the other a failure who had been able to achieve little save the writing of some children's stories. The successful brother was called to Berlin to receive a prestigious award and took the other brother with him, hoping the journey would help relieve the brother's depression. When the train arrived, the official delegation on the platform began to issue the formal greeting. Suddenly there was a noise. We look and see a child running down the street toward them. No, it's two children. No, five. No, twenty-five. No, five hundred! Children running, climbing over fences, swinging out of trees, coming through large drainpipes and around corners on their way to the station. And what's that they're saying? "We want a story! We want a story!" The historian turns with a smile to his dumbfounded brother and motions him forward. "We want a story," the children continue. Finally, the brother, who had thought himself a failure, raised his arms and began, "Once upon a time there were two brothers..."[25]

Creative contemporary people with philosophical underpinnings as widely different as filmmaker Stephen Spielberg and cultural theologian Tex Sample echo that scene from the story of the Brothers Grimm and agree that what we must have to communicate in today's world are not the latest special effects or other technological gimmickry, but good stories. Many of the most powerful stories in the Bible are gathered in the book of Judges. Are they good stories? That depends. They are certainly not happy stories, but they are provocative and compelling ones. Earlier I mentioned how one of them has haunted me for more than a quarter-century. Few if any contemporary stories have that kind of punch.

Furthermore, it has been said that church is the only public place where it is socially acceptable to sleep. Many people, especially young people, do not like to listen to preaching because they find it boring and soporific. They tend to be visual learners and quickly check out of droning abstractions from talking heads. Well, Judges is certainly not boring. And it is a very visual book. As one reads or listens to these stories, one sees them! And responds. With surprise, laughter, shock, horror, whatever. Finally, since most of our people are unfamiliar with these stories, they do not carry with them any preconceived baggage about the text. When the scripture is announced, people do not groan inwardly, "Oh, no, not again," because they have never been there. With the exception of Samson and Delilah, and possibly Deborah and Gideon, most of our people could not name a single character upon the stage of Judges' action. This gives us the chance to preach some very contemporary messages based on some very old and yet new stories.

CHAPTER 2

The Failed Conquest of Canaan

Judges 1:1–2:5

The book of Judges begins by reminding us that the conquest of Canaan was not completed by Joshua. Military operations continued after his death. The 1:1–2:5 passage recounts the defeat and mutilation of Canaanite king Adonibezek (1:1–7); successful initial forays against Jerusalem and Hebron (1:8–10); the story of Caleb, Othniel, and Achsah, and the victory over Debir (1:11–15); further victories over other cities, with the exception of Jerusalem, which would not taken until the time of David (1:16–21); a spy story reminiscent of the Rahab story in Joshua 2 (1:22–26); and a final section that details the failure of the conquest. The indigenous peoples for the most part were not driven out (1:27–36). This is explained in 2:1–5 as a failure of faith. Several interesting stories at the beginning of the book can profitably be engaged homiletically.

One of the concerns that immediately faces the preacher is that most of the stories in Judges concern military enterprises. Some preachers and congregations are comfortable with sermons that have a military motif; some are not. But no one can deny that most of the problems that face us today—as individuals, congregations, societies—have an "us" versus "them" quality. And the stories in Judges reach beneath the battles themselves to the social and theological issues that are involved in human conflict. One does not have to preach from Judges with sword in hand; one does often have to preach from Judges with heart in hand.

21

Adonibezek: Dehumanizing Your Enemies (Judges 1:1–7)

One of the most important and valuable professions of our time is that of conflict mediation. To live is to come into conflict with others, intentionally or unintentionally. I was driving down the street not long ago when two people in a pickup truck pulled up beside me. The driver was honking his horn, and the passenger was shaking his fist at me through the window. We came to a stop sign. I rolled down my window and said, "Did I do something that made you angry?" The man seemed to be disarmed by this and finally said, "Yeah, you cut us off back there." "I'm very sorry," I said. "I never saw you." "Well, OK," he said, as they sped up and left. I breathed a sigh of relief. I live in a state where it is now legal to carry concealed handguns. I had no idea whether or not the people in the truck had a gun, and I was glad the conflict was defused quickly. Many such conflicts are not. With the growth of "road rage," little conflicts can escalate to shouting matches and even violence.

Whether or not our conflicts can be mediated often depends not only on the solutions offered, but also on how we treat those with whom we are in conflict. When we treat our opponents badly, when we dehumanize them, when, in contemporary parlance, we disrespect–or "diss"–them, chances of resolution are lessened. I hold in my hand this week's local newspaper. One letter writer says that his adversary is that "last bastion of ignorance…a bottom-feeding politician."[1] How soon do you think that conflict will be resolved?

The book of Judges begins by immediately living up to its reputation as a gruesome book. In the continuing conquest of Canaan, the Israelites defeat the Canaanites and Perizzites, who were under the leadership of King Adonibezek. The king escapes but is captured. He is not killed, at least not immediately. Rather, his thumbs and big toes are cut off. He is then quoted as having said, "Seventy kings with their thumbs and big toes cut off used to pick up scraps under my table; as I have done, so God has paid me back" (1:7). I very much doubt the accuracy of this quotation, but we can see what is being suggested by the writer: a demonstration of the Mosaic code "eye for eye, tooth for tooth,"[2] and, we suppose, thumb for thumb and toe for toe.

Adonibezek was not, of course, a Hebrew. Applying this code to him may have been part of the Israelites' conquest strategy. To the victors go the spoils, and one of the spoils is setting up your legal system in the place of the system of the conquered people. But this is opprobrious behavior, the only story in the Bible in which Israel mutilated an enemy. It is so jarring that we are reminded that "no political order or ideology, whether of Joshua or Judah or judges or kings can escape responsibility or judgment under God's ultimate rule."[3]

What the Israelites did to Adonibezek was to dehumanize him as he had done to others. Without our big toes, we cannot stand erect and walk. Without the opposable thumb, we cannot make tools and other products, much less make war. These activities, along with language, separate us from the rest of the animal world. With thumbs and big toes cut off, we have been reduced to subhuman level. We rejoice in the development of electronic devices and patterns of loving caregiving that enable people to overcome injuries like this today, but they had no such devices or care three thousand years ago.

Yes, the king reaped what he sowed. But so did the Israelites. By treating the king as they did, by dehumanizing the Canaanite leader, the Israelites almost assured that the two peoples would have a very difficult time living together in peace. Imagine Ulysses S. Grant cutting off Robert E. Lee's thumbs and toes at Appomattox. How would that have affected the healing between North and South? And how does the history of mutilations in the Middle East, from Adonibezek to the latest children who have lost limbs to land mines or suicide bombers, affect the possibilities for peace? Think about this the next time you are tempted to road rage, racial injustice, or the desire to show somebody up or to put somebody down.

Goodbye to the City of Books (Judges 1:11–13)

Just across the border from England sits the little Welsh village of Hay-on-Wye. Because of its strategic location, it has been the site of many battles. It was captured during the Norman invasion and destroyed by King John in 1216. The town and its castle were again destroyed in 1265, 1322, and 1453. We might say Hay-on-Wye did not have much luck defending itself.

Finally, the town, weary of being cannon fodder for successive armies, took a different tack and gained a new personality. A man named Richard Booth opened a bookstore in the decrepit castle. Other booksellers came, and now, many years later, the tiny village of Hay-on-Wye is the largest venue in the world for secondhand and rare books. Over thirty major booksellers have set up shop there, and bibliophiles from around the world make pilgrimage to the village known round the world as the "town of books." The change in focus from war to books changed the life and reputation of Hay-on-Wye. We wish the "town of books" well.[4]

We also remember when it did not go so well. Perhaps the greatest tragedy in Western intellectual history was the torching by Julius Caesar of the library at Alexandria in Egypt in 47 B.C.E. The library had claimed a copy of every scroll known to its administrators. How and why it was destroyed is the stuff of legend; all we know for sure is that the library and all its scrolls disappeared. Among the works presumed lost was Aristotle's second book of *Poetics.* It remains a fact that wars do not destroy only armies but libraries as well, and with them, culture and civilization. Why were the Dark Ages dark? In large measure because they lost their books. I remember that during the Cold War one scholar reminded us how one of the never-mentioned but critical losses to humankind in a nuclear war would be the destruction of thousands and thousands of libraries, towns and cities of books, as it were.[5]

On April 25–27, 1992, early in the Balkan war, Serbian nationalists bombarded the National Library in Sarajevo with incendiary grenades, reducing the library to ashes and in the process wiping out nearly the entire written record of Bosnia's history.[6] Most recently, the September 11, 2001, terrorist attack on the World Trade Center in New York City not only killed thousands of people and destroyed a center of international commerce but also destroyed millions of dollars' worth of art. Irreplaceable works by artists such as Alexander Calder, Louise Nevelson, Joan Miro, and Roy Lichtenstein were lost. In the words of Sally Webster, professor of art history at New York's City University, it was "an attack on our very culture and civilization."[7]

As the "conquest" of Canaan continued after the death of Joshua, Caleb ordered the taking of the city of Debir, formerly known as Kiriath-sepher. And why did the Israelites change the name of the city from Kiriath-sephir to Debir? Danna Nolan Fewell has a devastating answer:

> Kiriath-sephir is, literally, "the city of writing" or "the city of books"…The place to be destroyed is a center of learning: a place where records are kept, where history and order are valued, a place where texts are produced…Even when one's allegiances lie with the Israelites, the loss of such culture may give the reader pause.[8]

Lillian Klein suggests the city could also have been a center of Canaanite religion.[9] The city to be razed was then a center of culture and religion. Its loss would have been tragic for the Canaanites and for those today who want to understand them better. Contrary to this picture of destruction, the Bible does not always rejoice when foreign cultures and religions are destroyed. The lament in Revelation 18 over the fall of Babylon is an example. Babylon was rife with sin and had to go, but good things in Babylon also would be lost; it was a city of great cultural splendor. So there was sadness when it fell.[10]

The point here is simple. In warfare not only do political ideologies rise and fall, not only is ground taken or lost, not only are people killed, but also the cultural and intellectual life of peoples and nations is often severely damaged if not destroyed. Here at the beginning of the conquest of Canaan, the City of Books was taken and probably destroyed. The intellectual and religious center of a people's life was laid waste. At the end of the Bible the destruction of Babylon (read: Rome), a great center of learning, is predicted. From beginning to end, we are reminded how fragile are the intellectual and spiritual lives of people, how susceptible to destruction from without and within.

Defend your land, yes. But do not forget to take care of your books. And be merciful to your enemy's books as well as to your enemy.

Achsah and the Blessing of an Imperfect Land (Judges 1:11–15)

For a person mentioned in only a few verses of scripture,[11] Achsah has certainly captured much attention of contemporary scholars.[12] What does the text tell us? Caleb offered his daughter Achsah in marriage to whoever could capture the city of Debir. Othniel did so, and Achsah was given to him as wife. She was a trophy of war, who also carried a name that meant "bangle" or "anklet." Her name reminds us of Job's daughters, who were named "turtledove," "cinnamon," and "a box of eye shadow." Not exactly names bearing *gravitas*. And we are not prepared to expect much of Achsah. Then come two curious verses (14–15), where Achsah suddenly acted not like a trophy taken in war, but like a self-assertive person.

She encouraged her husband to ask for land and then approached her father with an additional request: "Give me a blessing."[13] She asked for springs of water, which may mean springs to water the arid Negeb land she and Othniel had received, or may, according to Lillian Klein, have sexual connotations, much like Jacob's request in Genesis 32.[14] But why must one read Achsah sexually when we do not so read Jacob? I would prefer to read Achsah's request more literally as acting on her realization that to survive in an arid land she and her family would have to have water.[15]

Exodus 3:7–8 has God say:

> I have observed the misery of my people who are in Egypt; I have heard their cry on account of their taskmasters. Indeed, I know their sufferings, and I have come down to deliver them from the Egyptians, and to bring them up out of that land to a good and broad land, a land flowing with milk and honey.

One might thus expect the Holy Land to be modeled after the garden of Eden: lush, green, beautiful. Two things surprised me on my first trip to the Holy Land. The first was what a small piece of ground this is in relation to its great importance, politically and religiously. The entire country of Israel could be placed in the Dallas/Fort Worth metroplex with room left over. The second is that the primary crop of this land "flowing with milk and honey" is rocks.

I have heard it suggested that the first time Achsah looked at the land she had been given, she mumbled, "We left Egypt for this?" Three thousand years later Israeli Prime Minister Golda Meir would lament the fact that Moses and Joshua had led the Israelites to the only land in the Middle East that had no oil. But this is a story about water.

In dry areas such as the southwestern United States there are water-related sayings: "Water does not run downhill; it runs toward money," and "Whiskey is for drinking; water is for fighting over." The great Colorado River, for example, no longer even reaches the sea, sucked dry before it can get there. This theme of precious water is the touchstone of John Nichols's powerful novel *The Milagro Beanfield War*. Early on, we read how the "war" began:

> Milagro itself was half a ghost town, and all the old west side beanfields were barren, because over thirty-five years ago, during some complicated legal and political maneuverings known as the 1935 Interstate Water Compact, much of Milagro's Indian Creek water had been reallocated to big-time farmers down in the southeast portion of the state or in Texas, leaving folks like Joe Mondragon high and much too dry.[16]

So it was that one day

> Joe suddenly decided to irrigate [his] little field and grow himself some beans. It was that simple. And yet irrigating that field was an act as irrevocable as Hitler's invasion of Poland...or the assassination of the Archduke Ferdinand, because it was certain to catalyze tension which had been building for years, certain to precipitate a war.[17]

Achsah, like Joe, knew that water is life. People go to war for it. But while men fight over water and take it for their own use, this woman—who two verses earlier was a war prize, an ornament—called water a blessing and asked for it. This action serves as a counterpoint to most of the other action in Judges. Perhaps the writer is saying to the first readers and to us, "If everyone else in this book had acted like Achsah, we would have had a very different story to tell." She came to a dry and imperfect land and sought the blessing that would give life to that land.

We too live in an imperfect land. Seek the blessings of God that give life. Ask and they will be given unto you.

Indigenous Peoples (Judges 1:19–33)

The stories of one people's trying to drive another out of the latter's homeland are prime motifs of human history. What history often neglects to tell us, however, is that these efforts almost always fail. From Hitler's demand for *Lebensraum* to Milosevich's ethnic cleansing, and then back to the biblical story of the Israelites' attempts to drive the inhabitants out of the "promised land," we find history littered with failures to dislodge indigenous peoples. These peoples may have been conquered militarily; they may have been (as the saying goes) silenced but not converted; they may even have been enslaved, but they remain. Why?

Some may remain in their ancestral homelands under the most stringent oppression believing that what comes around goes around—that someday things will be made right. But many others simply do not see any option; they have literally no place else to go, and their attachment to their home is strong. Recently we were saddened to see on television an old woman climbing from the ruins of her home in Grozny, capital of Chechnya, after the Russians had finally driven the Chechnyan rebels from their capital. "Where do we go now?" she asked. "What do we do now?" How many hundreds of thousands of times have those questions been voiced in human history?

People who know little or nothing about the Bible will know little or nothing about the so-called conquest of Canaan. Those who know more probably assume that the Israelites drove out the inhabitants of Canaan with dispatch. The truth is—at least the truth told by the book of Judges—that the Israelites never succeeded in driving out the inhabitants of the land. The writer assumed that since God had "given" this land to the Israelites,

God wanted the indigenous people to be driven out. That they were not must be chalked up to some failure on the part of the Israelites, which we find out in chapter 2 is the case. The Israelites mingled with the people of the land, displeasing God. This suggestion displeases the writer of this book, making God appear to be one I would not want to worship. From my perspective, this is pure excuse-making and not very convincing.[18] I shall leave this thinking to its own reward, but I do want to pick up on the writer's repetitions of the failures. Consider the following:

- v. 19: "The LORD was with Judah, and he took possession of the hill country, but could not drive out the inhabitants of the plain, because they had chariots of iron."
- v. 21: "the Benjaminites did not drive out the Jebusites who lived in Jerusalem."
- v. 27: "Manasseh did not drive out the inhabitants of Beth-shean."
- v. 28: "When Israel grew strong, they put the Canaanites to forced labor, but did not in fact drive them out."
- v. 29: "And Ephraim did not drive out the Canaanites who lived in Gezer."
- v. 30: "Zebulon did not drive out the inhabitants of Kitron."
- v. 31: "Asher did not drive out the inhabitants of Acco."
- v. 33: "Naphtali did not drive out the inhabitants of Beth-shemesh."

This recitation does two things. First, the tendency to think about the stories in Judges as Israelite versus Canaanite may be misguided. More and more scholars today suggest that the Israelites must be understood as Canaanites. Susan Ackerman writes, for example, that "the Israelites, no matter how diligently they sought to distinguish themselves from Canaanite cultures like those of Ugarit and Phoenicia, were in fact of Canaanite descent."[19]

Second, if this does nothing else for us, it should move us to consider the place and plight of indigenous peoples and the horror of slavery. For those of us who live in North America, it calls attention to those now called Native Americans or First People. They have been called many other things, of course, most of them derogatory. But European Americans did not drive them out. They are still here. And we have become a part of them. We are all Canaanites.

CHAPTER 3

The Rise of the Judges

Judges 2:6–3:31

Joshua and his entire generation died. Without Joshua's strong faith and charismatic leadership, the people immediately fell into apostasy and worshiped other gods. The LORD[1] was angered by this and "gave them over to plunderers" and "sold them into the power of their enemies" (2:14). Then the LORD raised up judges to deliver the people, but as soon as the crisis abated, the Israelites relapsed into sin. So the LORD decided not to drive out their enemies. All the peoples and nations that remained were, as the text says, "for the testing of Israel" (3:4).

The main homiletical question to be engaged in this section is whether or not God tests us. At the end of the previous section, the angel of the LORD warned the Israelites that the other gods of the other people in the land would be a snare to them. The people called the place where the angel rebuked them Bochim, the place of "weepers." Like us, the Israelites rejoiced in a God who loved them unequivocally; they were less thrilled with a God who criticized them for their sins. Some have even suggested that Judges might be called "a book of weeping."[2] Many among us could also write such a book.

God's testing of people has never made good theological sense to me. The idea behind the book of Job, that Job's family and flocks are killed, that everything he has is taken from him, including his health, all as the result of a stupid wager between God and Satan, is preposterous. The point of the book, that there is no simple answer to the question of suffering, is well

31

taken. But the plot is awful and certainly not to be taken seriously.

Similarly, I have never thought of dread diseases, car wrecks, tornadoes, terrorist attacks, and the like as God's way of testing us.[3] On the other hand, God has done something with us that might be construed a test. God has given us our freedom. God did not have to do that. It would have been easier and a lot less trouble for God to have kept us as puppets. But then God would not have been able to live in relationship with us and we with God. You cannot relate to a puppet. With the freedom that God gave us comes the opportunity to live well or poorly, to pass or fail the test that freedom is. In this text and most of the book of Judges, the Israelites, brought up out of Egypt into freedom, fail that test —as we do with regularity. This may be one reason why the ancient Hebrews and the people of today are so dependent on and grateful for God's mercy and forgiveness.

God Has No Grandchildren (Judges 2:7–10)

The problems that are going to cover the Israelites like a mudslide are foreshadowed in this text. Joshua died; so did Joshua's whole generation. The people worshiped the LORD all the days of Joshua and saw the great work that the LORD had done for Israel (2:7). But after Joshua's generation passed from the scene, another generation grew up "who did not know the LORD or the work that the LORD had done for Israel" (2:10). So whose fault is that? In the following chapters of Judges the succeeding generations are going to be blamed for all manner of theological and ethical malfeasance. Our legal system says that ignorance of the law is no excuse for committing a crime. It may be no excuse, but it is a terrible shame. Similarly, when one has never been taught about God, it is very hard to know God. You may be blamed for that, as the generations after Joshua were, but I suggest that what we have here is a failure of religious education. "Train children in the right way," says Proverbs 22:6, "and when old, they will not stray." One wonders if the writer had the disastrous period of the judges in mind.

In Numbers 32 God determined that the older generation was not to enter the land, only those born on the journey from

Egypt. Now even those are gone. And the remaining people "abandoned the LORD, the God of their ancestors" (2:12). God has no grandchildren.

Why Do People Change Gods? (Judges 2:16-23)

In this unusual text, we find people changing gods as one might change toothpastes. This is a puzzle to me. The god-engram develops in our brains from an early age. As we mature, our god-images tend to grow with us, moving beyond the old grandfather to something more universal. But few people throw away the whole concept of the god with which they have grown up.

In Joshua and Judges, the people frequently appear to abandon the LORD, who brought them up out of Egypt. Why? When I was a young pastor in California, I would frequently call on people we hoped might be interested in the church. Were they church members? Yes. Where? First Church in Sioux City, Iowa. And when they went back home to visit relatives, they went to church. But they did not go to church in southern California. Church, and by extension God, were part of their past, but not their present, and probably not their future, unless they moved back to the Midwest or had some theophany that shook them from their spiritual lethargy. It is fascinating to look at a county-by-county map of the United States that is color-coded according to the percentage of the population that claims a church relationship. The map shows that with the exception of New Mexico and Utah, the country becomes increasingly pagan as one moves west.

I suspect something similar was at work among the Israelites. When they were suffering under the yoke of Pharaoh, the LORD was a very present help in trouble. But how soon all of us forget when the burdens are lifted from us. Moses led the children of Israel out of Egypt across the parted Red Sea, which then drowned their pursuers, surely the most incredible display of divine power in human history. Three days later—three days!—the people were complaining about this and that. Amazing.

Now in Canaan, with no one alive who saw those mighty acts of God, the people were quite willing to abandon the LORD for Canaanite gods. They probably remembered the LORD from the campfire stories about their deliverance. But the exodus was in the past, like the days back in Sioux City. Why do people change or abandon gods? Because of business or politics. Because a different god either appears more impressive or makes easier demands on them. Because the god of their past has been "absent" for a long time. But mostly, I believe, people abandon God and church because they never established a strong relationship with God, because the hook was never set in them. Again, in an age when religious education seems to have fallen on hard times, we see just how important it is.

Othniel: The Good Judge (Judges 3:7–11)

The first major judge hardly seems so. Othniel's story is told in a spare five verses. But his story is important beyond its brevity, for within it is found the pattern for the cycle that will be repeated throughout the book.

1. "The Israelites did what was evil in the sight of the LORD" (3:7).[4]
2. The LORD in anger gave them into the power of an enemy (3:8).
3. "The Israelites cried out to the LORD" (3:9a).
4. "The LORD raised up a deliverer for the Israelites" (3:9b).
5. The deliverer with the LORD's aid defeated the enemy (3:10).
6. "The land had rest" during the rest of the deliverer's life (3:11).[5]

As the cycle was reenacted in the lives of other judges, they tended to fall short of the model leader exemplified by Othniel. Was Othniel really such a good judge? We do not know. While some great leaders fall into undeserved obscurity, others, less worthy, have the benefit of good memorializers and find a place in history.

I like, for example, the story of Saint Cuthbert (ca. 633–687), the best-loved saint of northeastern England. After visiting his tomb in Durham Cathedral, I read about his life. In his youth he was a gamester, a shepherd, and perhaps a soldier. After a vision, he became a monk, a prior, a hermit, and a bishop, before returning to an island hermitage to spend his last days in prayer and meditation. A biographer says that Cuthbert became the best-known and best-loved saint of the north of England "not because of anything special he did, but because of what he was."[6] And what was he? As best I can tell, he was a nice fellow in a not-very-nice time. He loved God, nature, people. They say that in the land of the blind, the one-eyed man is king. We might add that in a rotten time, the nice fellow is a saint, that in a time of social and religious disintegration, a good judge is long remembered. This is not to say, "Be good and you will be remembered." Goodness is its own reward. Others may remember or not. God will never forget the good you have done.

So it happened that the Israelites sinned and were given into the hand of King Cushan-rishathaim of Aram-naharaim for eight years. The king's name in Hebrew means "Cusan of Double Wickedness," an "obviously villainous and perhaps satirical royal name for which we have no record."[7] Othniel defeated the doubly wicked king, and the land had rest for forty years.[8] And people remembered.

Ehud and Eglon: Murder in the Toilet (Judges 3:12–30)

In this story Israel again did what was evil in the sight of the LORD and as a result was given into the hand of Eglon, king of the Moabites (though the text says that he only captured the city of Jericho). After eighteen years of subjection, a deliverer arose in the person of Ehud, a left-handed Benjaminite. Taking tribute to the king, he hid a short dagger on his right thigh, cajoled the king's attendants into a private audience with Eglon, and there in the king's "cool chamber" stabbed Eglon—whose name could mean "fat calf"—in his ample belly so that the excrement poured out of the dying king.[9] The king's court, waiting in the antechamber, assumed from the smell that the king was relieving himself. Ehud escaped—some say through the toilet itself—before the attendants finally came in and found the king dead. Then Ehud rallied his troops and defeated the Moabites, killing ten thousand of them and ushering in eighty years of peace.

Most of the problems to be encountered in a journey through the world of the judges are anticipated in this short story. The hero is a sinister assassin who carries out his mission in a tale laden with ethnic, scatological, and perhaps sexual humor. Picture generations of Israelites sitting around the campfire as the teller of tales recounts the story of how brave Ehud tricked the stupid, fat Moabites and conquered them. This cruel (to us) and off-color (to us) story is inevitably received with rollicking laughter and ethnic pride.

Questions leap at us. What happened here? That is far from clear. These few verses are loaded with *hapax legomena,* words that appear nowhere else in scripture and are consequently hard to define. Some scholars argue that the story is fiction;[10] others believe it has a historical basis.[11] So we are left not only unclear about the language of the story but unsure whether we are dealing with a historical event at all. As one writer argues, "Neither Ehud nor Eglon is a possible personal name of the late second millennium or first millennium B.C.E."[12] He goes on to suggest that Ehud was not a Benjaminite leader, but a clan, and that Eglon was not a king, but a Canaanite toponym or place name.

This leads to the second question, one we shall be tempted to ask again and again as we work our way through Judges: what is this story doing in the Bible? The idea of God's using assassins to achieve God's purposes is offensive to most people, and the fact that we find ethnic, put-down humor and toilet jokes in scripture is also rather distasteful. Scholars have gone through a variety of contortions to answer this question. We are reminded that the "left-handed" ways of God are not our ways.[13] Well, I should hope not. But I find little value or solace in the argument that God is free to act morally worse than we do. Some time ago, I attended an ordination service at which the choir sang an anthem that affirmed:

> The Lord my God is sovereign…
> God can do whatever He wants to do,
> where He wants to,
> how He wants to…
> Who am I to question His wisdom (I am nothing).

Who am I to question His judgments (I am nothing).[14]

As a guest, I bit my lip and kept silence. Had I had more chutzpah, I might have stood up and asked: "Can we talk about that?"

Others have taken a different theological tack by suggesting that because the Moabites were interfering with God's right to this land—"God's own country"—the murder of Eglon and the put-down of the Moabites were justified.[15] Has there ever been a war, or even a battle, in human history in which each and every side did not claim to be fighting, not for themselves, but rather for "God"? A few perhaps, but not many. There was a time when I argued vigorously against the concept of military chaplaincy because I believed that serving within the command structure of the military placed ordained ministers in an untenable theological position. I finally gave up my opposition because of another, less abstract concern. Most of the people in military service around the world are young, many away from home for the first time, and they need the ministry of dedicated chaplains more than I need my theological position vindicated. Even so, I still bristle when violence is perpetrated in the name of God.

Another argument is more complicated, with a slant from liberation theology. This argument suggests that oppressed people have certain rights in the sight of God that oppressors do not. Violence by the oppressed is thus not sinful to the same degree that violence by oppressors is. The classic modern case is that of Dietrich Bonhoeffer, a great Christian and a pivotal figure in twentieth-century ethics. Bonhoeffer joined the resistance against the Nazis and even participated in an assassination attempt against Hitler. He finally came to realize that "anyone who was not ready to kill Hitler was guilty of mass murder, whether he liked it or not."[16] The situation, for Bonhoeffer, and perhaps for Ehud and the author of Judges, suggested that the death of one man might save the lives of many. If we are quick to agree with this, we must also remember that this was Caiaphas's argument for the death of Jesus in John 11: It is expedient for one man to die that the whole nation should not perish. I understand this argument, but I remain very uncomfortable with it.

Similarly, this argument suggests that the oppressed have a license to poke fun at their oppressors, a license that is not reciprocal. Not long ago I was worshiping with a congregation where a respected but past-his-prime interim minister was holding forth. He concluded his sermon with these words, "Like the old darky said, 'I'se jus' doin' the bes' I can.'" The congregation was stunned. The hymn began, but no one stood until, finally, we straggled to our feet, looking at one another. In the narthex after the service, I heard one woman say to another, "No, he just couldn't have said that. He must have said, 'Like old Dorothy said.'" This average European American audience knew that a boundary had been crossed, a rule violated. I have books in my office about early twentieth-century American oratory that are filled with examples just like the one the preacher used. But they belong to another time, and the wrongheaded permission to use them has long since expired. Had an African American preacher told a story about crackers or honkies in a black congregation, I cannot be sure, but I doubt the reaction would have been so negative. I am aware that we are teetering on the edge of the debate about so-called "political correctness," and I have no desire to fall in. So let me conclude this part by saying that although I can appreciate the argument that grants to the oppressed or marginalized a license for ethnic humor that is denied to oppressors and marginalizers, I still feel that making fun of groups of people, be they Moabites or Israelites, African or European Americans, gay or straight, the able-bodied or persons with physical disabilities, or any other sets of groups, tells us more about the persons making fun than those being made fun of.[17] And one of the things mockery tells us is that their vision is narrow and skewed. When it comes to a biblical text like this, care must also be exercised. In biblical scholar Lowell K. Handy's words,

> Most [sic] biblical scholars know no Moabites; moreover, it is traditional for faith communities to read

these stories through the eyes of the Judean authors. We laugh, or smirk superiorly, along with the author as the dumb Moabites "get theirs," safe in the knowledge that no present-day Moabite Anti-Defamation League is going to object.[18]

The Bible is generally forthright about just rewards. Pharaoh oppressed the Hebrews, then lost his son and his army.[19] Judas betrayed Jesus, then went and hanged himself. Since there is no evidence in the text that Eglon was a cruel ruler,[20] one that deserved his humiliating assassination, we might expect a *quid pro quo* later in Israelite-Moabite history. Such never happened. In fact the Moabite people and religion would become extinct, and the land of Moab a depopulated wasteland for centuries.[21] However, we may be too quick in our look for a historical balancing of the scales, since the odds are significantly in favor of this story being the stuff of legend. Better that we look within the text itself. If we do, we soon notice the relatedness of the Ehud and Samson stories. Both are heroes of the trickster genre. Both stories make use of irony and humor. But the ethnic humor of the Ehud story has been reversed. The stupidity of Eglon and the Moabites allows Ehud and the Israelites to triumph, but, in Handy's words, Samson is "strong, handsome, virile, lusty, and dumb as a rock."[22] The Moabite king has metamorphosed into the last judge of Israel. And what goes around does in fact come around.

So what do we do with this text? Two compelling suggestions have been made by Lowell Handy and Ferdinand Deist. Handy, in urging that the story not be taken literally, says that if we accept ethnic stereotyping as approved for interpreting the Bible, then the legitimation of depersonalization has been achieved. We must realize, he says, that the Moabites are used in this story as stick figures and not as real people.[23] There is some comfort in that. But lest we get too comfortable, Handy reminds us that the realization that our Bible contains not just ethnic humor, but ethnic humor of the most vicious kind, is not an easy one to make. What must we do? Accept it, he says, and deal with it.

Deist suggests that two lessons may be learned from this text. The first is that we should deduce, from extreme examples such as the Ehud story, that the *whole* Bible suffers from its cultural embeddedness and is, therefore, in need of more than mere translation.[24] Simply to translate such stories into Western theological categories is to suggest that brutal violence is justified as part of some divine plan. But what do we gain in saying to our people that yes, God does employ assassins and, yes, assassination is wrong, and if they cannot understand that, it is because ancient oriental and modern Western worldviews are different?

Here is the rub. Although I was constantly reminded when I was in seminary to exegete the text (let it speak for itself out of its own context) and not eisegete the text (read my own views into it), we now live in a scholarly world where exegesis and eisegesis have alloyed and disappeared under the broader and more fluid label of interpretation. One new interpretative tool is reader-response criticism, with similarities to the old eisegesis that we were warned about. So while I appreciate Deist's warning not to see this story through our eyes, there is a sense in which these are the only eyes we have. Our people are not going to look at the text through an ancient Near Eastern mind-set, and could not even if they wished to do so. Therefore, if we cannot make this story live in the place where we live, we cannot preach it with any effect. The key here, I believe, is to ask what functions in our world in the same way this story functioned in its world. I immediately think of the scene in the motion picture *Philadelphia* where Tom Hanks, playing a lawyer who is a closeted gay man, is sitting in a sauna with other lawyers and is forced to laugh when one of them tells a gay joke. The sauna was not Eglon's bathroom, but it was close. The joke was not Ehud's dagger, but it was close.

The second suggestion that Deist makes is that we should take the *strangeness* of the biblical witness seriously, which, in turn, should make us aware of the strangeness and peculiarity of our own theological concoctions.[25] He is certainly correct about that.

I do not suspect that many preachers would use this text, in full detail, as the basis for a sermon, though I can imagine certain places and occasions where it might be appropriate: in a setting where a group of people have been depersonalized or stigmatized in the name of God because of who they are and because of the perpetrators' literal use of biblical texts like this one to justify their actions. I think, moreover, that the story could be useful as supportive material in sermons dealing with justice themes such as ethnic stereotyping, ethnic humor, or the strangeness of the theological enterprise. What follows are four homiletical vignettes so constructed.

Seeing Yourself in the Eyes of Others (Judges 3:12–17)

In a 1989 pilot episode for a television series called *Sister Kate,* a nun makes it clear to two African American orphans that she would not tolerate stereotypes, especially about nuns:

Violet: Are you really a nun?

Sister Kate: Yes, child.

Neville: Then where's your guitar?

Sister Kate: I don't know. Where are your tap shoes? You see, Neville, we must learn not to think in terms of stereotypes. Just because a person is black doesn't mean to say he can tap dance, and just because a person happens to be a nun doesn't mean she sings or plays guitar. (Pause) Or, incidentally, likes children.[26]

Sister Kate is correct. We learn to stereotype and we must also learn not to do so. What she does not say is how much harder the latter is than the former. To unlearn racism, sexism, homophobia, xenophobia, and other ways of stereotyping persons is very difficult. Especially when we find such practice accepted, even praised, in the Bible. In the book of Judges, for example, enemies of the Israelites are often caricatured, such as the king of the Moabites, whom they call Eglon the Fat.

African American religious leader L. Wayne Stewart tells a story from his own childhood that points out the danger of such stereotyping and the way to see beyond it.

One Saturday morning me and my cousin Charles Fulbright and our best buddy Roy Scales were standing in front of the Texan movie theater in Clarksville, Texas, waiting to get our tickets for the picture show. One line would form in front of a sign that said, "Whites only," and another line would form in front of a sign that read "colored." It didn't matter how long you had been standing in the line marked "colored," because no one in the "colored" line was permitted to buy a ticket until everyone in the "Whites only" line got their ticket. So we were just standing there trying to be cool and act like we were not boiling with anger over having to stand in the hot sun while people in the "Whites only" line were driving up in air conditioned cars and going in ahead of us...

Just then this white boy named Billy Ray Bob Jackson bumped into me and said, "Git out of my way, nigger!" Well, I was not about to let him get away with that... so I shook my fist at him and said, "Billy Ray Bob Jackson— you white peckerwood—you can go around or go down this morning; it don't make me no difference."

Stewart describes a fight that only ended when both of the boys found themselves up in the air, held there by a police officer, who carted them off to jail. When they stood crying before a judge, the judge asked if they knew each other. "Yes," they sniffled.

The judge then said , "Billy Ray Bob Jackson, I want you to look into Louis Wayne Stewart's eyes and tell me what you see." Billy Ray Bob looked into my eyes and through more sobs and sniffs said, "I don't see nothing." "Well then, you got to get closer." And Billy Ray Bob moved his face closer to mine. "I still don't see nothing." "Well then, you got to get closer." This time Billy Ray Bob put his face right up next to mine and looked in my eyes. "What do you see now?" the judge said. And Billy Ray Bob said softly, "I see myself."[27]

If we could only get close enough to those with whom we disagree, we might not see our enemy at all, but rather ourselves. And that could change everything.

Ethnic Humor in the Church (Judges 3:20–22)

It is a fact of life that the vast majority of humor is put-down humor. We laugh at the weaknesses and foibles of others, getting our pleasure at their expense. We expect the objects of our humor either to be absent or to be tough-skinned enough to grin and bear it. If our humor is hurtful, oftentimes we never know it. A friend may not tell us her brother has AIDS or his sister has muscular dystrophy, even if our joke hurt her or him deeply. A lawyer friend may bear our lawyer joke with equanimity even if he or she is sick of such jokes. But all of us can remember times when we did not get away with inappropriate humor, when we told a hurtful story and were taken to task for it. "It was just a joke" is a feeble defense, and we end up chastened for a time.

Ethnic humor is a particularly troublesome and sometimes vicious type of put-down humor. And when it is used in church, the problem may be compounded. The story of Ehud and Eglon in Judges 3 does such compounding. Ehud kills Eglon, but that was not enough for the writer. We have to be informed that Eglon was fat, that Moabites were stupid, that Eglon was killed in the toilet, that he was gut-stabbed by Ehud, precipitating the release of excrement. A common, though deplorable, approach in such humor is to apply the language of one "otherness" to another "otherness" like female to race or, in this case, fat to foreigner.[28]

What can happen when we engage in ethnic humor like that? I remember an elder in a church who at every opportunity spoke about the centrality of love in the Christian gospel and the Christian life. He also never missed an opportunity to tell racist jokes. The result? His credibility with me and many people in the church was undermined, and his message of love fell on deaf ears.

So what can happen? Enemies can be made. Joke-tellers' words can hurt people. Credibility can be undermined. And so forth. In other words, not one good thing. It is a high price to pay for a few nervous titters.

Strangeness of the Theological Enterprise (Judges 3:23–25)

Every once in a while we read something in the Bible that astonishes us. We find, for example, unbelievable assertions, things that are theologically offensive, obvious exaggerations, vicious ethnic humor, and so forth.

Take for example, Psalm 137. What begins as sadness ends in anger as the psalmist writes one of the most difficult lines in the Bible: "Happy shall they be who take your little ones and dash them against the rock!" (137:9). That assertion is unacceptable under almost any theological veneer.[29]

Then there is Luke 14:25, an unbelievable assertion:

Now large crowds were traveling with him; and he turned and said to them: "Whoever comes to me and does not hate father and mother, wife and children, brothers and sisters, yes, and even life itself, cannot be my disciple."

Do you, gentle reader, hate your father and mother? hate your spouse and children? hate your brothers and sisters? Do you hate life itself? Jesus' words here are simply unbelievable.

Revelation 14:20 suggests that when the earth's harvest (that is, humanity) is reaped, blood will flow "as high as a horse's bridle for a distance of about two hundred miles." This is an obvious literary exaggeration. There is not that much blood on the planet.

Finally, let us not forget the scabrous ethnic humor found in the Ehud/Eglon story and elsewhere.

Several lessons can be found here. One, according to Ferdinand Deist, is that we must take the *strangeness* of the biblical witness to God seriously. What may have struck Israelite ears three thousand years ago, or first-generation Christian ears two thousand years ago, as perfectly reasonable may seem very strange to us. That should warn us that *our* theological assertions will no doubt seem strange to those who come after us. We should of course strive for the best theological understanding we can reach and then live faithfully in that understanding. But that is not the lesson here. The lesson is humility. Our answers to the great questions of life are not likely to be God's final—or even intermediate—answers. And we should not propound them as such. Rather, we say this is far as I can reach for now. And then we pray for God's mercy on our strange and shallow thought and for God's light on the road ahead.

"They Killed Everyone" (Judges 3:26–30)

A troublesome sidebar to the story of the unfinished conquest of Canaan trails from Joshua through Judges, and this comprises the various accounts that report that God gave such-and-such people or city into the Israelites' hand, and that they (the Israelites) slaughtered every single person in the town, presumably at God's behest. One example comes in 3:29, where "they killed about ten thousand of the Moabites, all strong, able-bodied men; no one escaped." I believe that God loves all people equally and that God loves them unconditionally. That being the case, I obviously cannot find support for my position in these writings. Is there anything to be learned from them at all?

Yes. Slaughter is contagious. Thirty-five years ago in Peace Corps training we raised chickens in preparation for our work in Africa. At the end of our program we had a feast. The menu was the vegetables and the chickens we had raised. A group of five of us were detailed to prepare the chickens. I had not done anything like that before and was squeamish in the early going. But soon I was ripping off the chickens' heads like everyone else. That I still remember the action with no little guilt shows the impact it made on me. Naturalist John Muir said it better. He was prevailed upon to join a hunt for Shasta wild sheep. One was wounded, and the hunters gave chase:

> In the excitement and savage exhilaration of the pursuit of the wounded, I, who have never killed any mountain life, felt like a wolf chasing the flying flock. But all this ferocity soon passed away, and we were Christians again.[30]

Blood lust is a powerful drug. And I wonder if the biblical accounts that attribute the slaughter of everyone to God's demand are not hiding this most dreadful of all addictions.

I teach my students what I have learned from David Buttrick, that it is always better to illustrate a positive point with a positive image and a negative point with a negative image.[31] What preachers often try to do is to illustrate a positive point with a negative image, either preceded or followed by some line like "Do not do it like this." There are times when one has no choice but to do that, no other images being available. Other times, however, when certain actions result in disaster, it is not unreasonable to move from bad action to bad result to positive point. This is what I believe happens in the book of Judges, whether it was the intention of the authors or not. This is our book now, and we can set the intention of the text up next to our theology and see which one is found wanting. If the text fails this test, we may have to find the courage—with fear and trepidation and humility—to preach the gospel against the text.

The Minor Judges: Narrative Sabbaths (Judges 3:31, 10:1–5, 12:8–13)

Minor surgery has been described as surgery being done on someone else. When it happens to us, it is "major," no matter how medically "minor." So what is a minor judge? Scholars have used several criteria to divide the major judges from the minor ones. Martin Noth, for example, suggested that the major judges were military heroes, while the minor judges were political figures in the amphictyony—a loose confederation of tribes—of Israel.[32] The presumption is that the editor of Judges took the so-called minor judges from an existing official record of Israelite magistrates.[33] Most scholars today have abandoned Noth's theory and suggest that distinctions between major and minor judges are made on the basis of the length and style of their accounts. For our purposes let us say simply that the minor judges are those about whom we know the least. These are the judges who have received the least ink. Thinking homiletically, I might say that the minor judges are those whose names you can be certain your people have never heard. I speak here of Shamgar, Tola, Jair, Ibzan, Elon, and Abdon.[34]

Four things we can say about these minor judges may be useful in present-day sermons. First, they serve to connect or contrast the stories that surround them. Second, they establish that the themes of peace and prosperity belong in the otherwise violent and unsettled story of this period in Israelite history. Third, they provide interludes in the midst of the intensity found in the major stories. And finally, they remind us that God is also the God of the blank spaces in the Bible. Consider each of these accomplishments.

The minor judges connect or contrast the stories on either side of them. For example, Shamgar, who is said to have "killed six hundred of the Philistines with an oxgoad" (3:31), comes between Ehud and Deborah/Jael who, like him, kill their enemies with unconventional weapons (two-edged sword and tent peg). The contrast is heightened when we realize that Shamgar may not even have been an Israelite.[35] Tola and Jair are paired between Gideon and Jephthah, with the peace and stability of their reigns in marked contrast to the warfare and strife of the "major" stories. And in the last three stories of Ibzan, Elon, and Abdon, set between the stories of Jephthah and Samson, the minor judges' great number of children and grandchildren contrast with the tragic death of Jephthah's only child and Samson's childlessness.[36]

The minor judges represent a time of peace and stability in an otherwise tumultuous period. If one were to read only the stories of the major judges, one would assume that the book tells of a time of unremitting hostility and disaster. This assumption would be wrong, for the few lines given to the minor judges speak of times of peace, stability, prosperity, and progeny. The rabbinic scholar Rashi says of Judges:

> Though the book's accounts of sin and war are lengthy, it records not a single event during the forty-year period of tranquility. In the context of the narrative it is clear that it was a time when the nation maintained the high standard of righteousness that the Torah demands. In fact, of the nearly four hundred years spanned by the period of the judges, the people were sinful during only one hundred and ten.[37]

This leads to the third achievement of the accounts of the minor judges. *The minor judges provide interludes to the intense stories of the major judges.* Let me explain the value of such interludes, both in scripture and in preaching. In the book of Revelation, for example, chapter 7 is an interlude between the sixth and seventh seals, and 10:1–11:13 forms an interlude between the sixth and seventh trumpets, respites before the intensity of the "sevenths." These interludes are more than "filler"; they give visions of the church and increase suspense before what is to come.[38]

Sermons are often structured like a bell curve, with a variety of pitch, volume, and speed making the content more hearable. When a preacher immediately moves into a fast, loud, high-pitched mode and stays there, segueing from point to point without pause, without rhetorical mercy, the listeners cannot long endure and will exit the train. *Saving Private Ryan*'s opening scene of the World War II landing at Omaha Beach consists of twenty-some minutes of the most intense film I have ever watched. When the scene finally ends, director Stephen Spielberg gently lets us down. He has to. We could not have sustained more.

Before we realized that many people today are visual learners and that embodied words—words that take on flesh—have much greater impact than disembodied conceptual language, preachers still understood that "illustrations" gave people a kind of mental respite or interlude from the abstractions of many dogmatic sermons. They were seen as a way of being kind to your people. During interludes, at the opera or at church, one does not have to focus or concentrate on the genre or theme of the music or sermon. So also for one reading or hearing read the book of Judges, twenty-six hundred years ago or today. The stories of the major judges are so intense and at times horrific that the interludes of the minor judges provide the mental rest necessary to continue. I remember reading a critique of Texas politics in which an old man reminded the author, "It ain't all bad, son." No, it is not. And the minor judges remind us of that.

The stories of the minor judges remind us that God is also God of the blank spaces in the Bible. A lot of stories are not fully recorded in scripture (for example, Jesus' doings between the ages of twelve and thirty). But scripture does take pains to remind us that God is in charge of the lacunae, of the untold stories. Olson writes of the relatively uneventful periods of the minor judges, "It is almost as if God needs this time to consider the options of what to do next with this people Israel who seem repeatedly inclined toward rebellion and self-destruction."[39]

This reminds us of the experience in Revelation 8:1, which says, "When the Lamb opened the seventh seal, there was silence in heaven for about half an hour." When someone asked what in the world that could mean, one person replied, "Maybe God needed some time to think." Well, if Olson is right, the same is at work in Judges. God, exasperated with the Israelites, needed some time to think. Hence the minor judges. Hence the time of relative inactivity. All quiet on the Canaanite front.

Deborah, Barak, and Jael

Judges 4–5

Someone altogether unfamiliar with the Bible, reading the gospels of Matthew and John, would soon realize that two writers are telling the same story in a different way. in the Hebrew Bible, 1 and 2 Kings and 1 and 2 Chronicles function similarly. As do chapters 4 and 5 of Judges. Here we have two renditions of the same tale, the first in prose and the second in poetry. The Song of Deborah in chapter 5 is regarded as one of the oldest pieces of literature in the Bible.[1] And the tale is fascinating. It begins as most of the other stories in Judges do. The Israelites sinned against God and consequently were given into the hand of King Jabin of Canaan, who oppressed them for twenty years.

A military leader named Barak arose. One expects more of the same kind of story found elsewhere in Judges. What one gets is unique in the Bible. Barak and his story are depreciated fore and aft by two women and their stories: Deborah and Jael.

Deborah is variously described by the text as a prophet, a mother in Israel, and either the "wife of Lappidoth" or a "woman of fiery torches" (read "spirited woman"), depending on the translation. She is further a singer of tales and a skilled poet, as we discover in chapter 5. The "mother in Israel" designation is particularly interesting. Deborah is the only biblical woman who did not attain that designation by being the mother of a famous son. We do not even know if she had

51

children. Her accomplishments were counsel, inspiration, and leadership. This description endured even to nineteenth-century America, where significant women were often eulogized as "mothers in Israel."

Deborah is generally viewed positively by everyone except pacifists. Even John Knox, in his venomous *First Blast of the Trumpet Against the Monstrous Regiment of Women*, said that:

> God, by privilege, favor, and grace, exempted Deborah from the common malediction given to women in that behalf; and against nature he made her prudent in counsel, strong in courage, happy in regiment, and a blessed mother and deliverer to his people.[2]

Deborah is often viewed as an extraordinary, rather than representative, woman, one who was not restricted by patriarchy, but who also did not stand over against it.[3] Others see her as a model of courage and power, a woman who risked her life to do the will of God, who shattered role expectations, and invites all of us to greater freedom.[4]

The other primary female character, Jael, has not been viewed so positively. Jael, the wife of Heber the Kenite, murdered the Canaanite general Sisera when he came to her for sanctuary. While Elizabeth Cady Stanton's *The Woman's Bible*, published in 1898, regarded Deborah as a "wise adviser," it had no kind words for Jael:

> The deception and the cruelty practiced on Sisera by Jael under the guise of hospitality is [*sic*] revolting under our code of morality. To decoy the luckless general fleeing before his enemy into her tent, pledging him safety, and with seeming tenderness ministering to his wants, with such words of sympathy and consolation lulling him to sleep, and then in cold blood driving a nail through his temple, seems more like the work of a fiend than of a woman.[5]

Leonard Swidler also calls Jael's act "a deceitful, cowardly assassination."[6] We shall later take issue with these calumnies and see why we perhaps should not consider Jael's act "under our code of morality."

For now we note that so many of the women in Judges are victims. It is interesting for us here to consider two who face risky situations and, rather than being overwhelmed, take charge of them.

"If You Will Not Go With Me" (Judges 4:4–9)

In my book on *Crisis Preaching* I tell the story from Exodus 33 in which Moses dickered with God about accompanying the children of Israel on their journey to the promised land. God did not want to go with them, saying "You are a stiff-necked people; if for a single moment I should go up among you, I would consume you" (33:5). At this point, Moses ran an extraordinary bluff, saying, "If your presence will not go, do not carry us up from here" (33:15).

This scene is reprised in Judges 4 with an interesting twist. This time the petitioner was Barak instead of Moses. Deborah said to Barak, a military leader from Naphtali, that God had commanded him to go into battle against Jabin's general Sisera, a battle that Barak would win. Barak was given a guarantee of victory from God (if he trusted the clairvoyance of Deborah). What more could a soldier want? Something more, obviously. In a reprise of the Moses story and a preview of the Gideon story, Barak said, "If you will go with me, I will go; but if you will not go with me, I will not go" (4:8). And the one being petitioned was not God, but Deborah.

Her answer was exquisite. "I will surely go with you; nevertheless, the road on which you are going will not lead to your glory, for the LORD will sell Sisera into the hand of a woman" (4:9). The writer wants us to believe that this is a reference to Deborah herself, which Barak did not seem to mind. Then we, and Barak, are surprised with the story of Jael, whose assassination of Sisera fulfills Deborah's prophecy and robs Barak of glory in the defeat of the Canaanites.

What then is the point of this story? That Barak is a coward? Perhaps. That the storyteller is clever? Perhaps. That glory in war is a fickle goal? Perhaps. But there is one more possibility concerning this text, the Moses story, and our own less adventurous lives: there are some things one just does not want to do alone. Maybe Barak just needed a comrade. I cannot hold that against him any more than I would chastise Moses for wanting to walk with God or a contemporary person for seeking the presence of God and human friends in her or his life.

I remember the time I took a group from church to a handbell festival. There were some talented soloists there whose hands were a blur as they played by themselves. But handbells are not made to be played alone. And the music of soloists cannot compare to the music generated by a full choir of bells. There are some things we do not want to do alone. The quest for the good and the true is among them. We have an answer to our problem today. We call it church.

Songs (Exodus 15:21, Judges 5:1–21, 1 Samuel 2:1–10, Luke 1:26–56)

The following dramatization, "Songs," could be staged as a play in a community hall, performed as readers' theater with chairs, or preached as a sermon in a clean chancel with no props at all.

First Narrator/Preacher: During the 1994 invasion of Haiti, Navy Lt. Comdr. Kenneth Carkhuff, a helicopter commander, informed his commanding officer that he would not go to sea because his religious and moral beliefs prevented him from going into combat with women. His unit, with two women pilots, went without him. Carkhuff said that "throughout the whole Bible, there are passages saying to protect and provide for the family. Part of that is you don't subject women to violence."[7] When pressed, Carkhuff admitted that "there are no specific scriptures that say women shall not serve in combat."[8]

Interestingly, the opposite is true, at least in the case of Deborah in chapters 4 and 5 of the book of Judges. She was the military leader, the brains and spirit behind the Israelites' defeat of the Canaanites under Sisera. One could claim that there is no evidence from the text that Deborah actually waded into combat with sword drawn. This is, with pun forgiven, beside the point. Using such an argument, one could also claim that General Eisenhower saw no combat in World War II. I must add that the text does not say Deborah did not participate in the violence, but whether she wielded a sword or not, Deborah was clearly in charge of the battle that day (4:9) and clearly gave the order that resulted in the deaths of thousands (4:14).

We are, most of us, uneasy with this. Priscilla Denham writes that the story "blows my condescending myth that women are more peaceful than men, that if women were put in positions of authority there would be less competition, less fighting, fewer wars in the world." In her words, "It's hard to sing to Song of Deborah."[9] Let us see just how hard it is.

Four women in the Bible are credited with songs, songs sung over a period of at least a thousand years.[10] But the songs have at least three things in common: they tell a story, they sing of overthrowing enemies, and they give praise to God. We might also wonder what, if anything, the women had in common. We can never really know that, but we can imagine. And in our imaginations perhaps we can see them and their stories recast as four young Southern women, living together in a cooperative apartment in New York City.

One door opens and then closes as a woman enters, walks to the front and stands there. She wears socks, leotards, and a sweatshirt.

Second Narrator: "Then the prophet Miriam, Aaron's sister, took a tambourine in her hand; and all the women went out after her with tambourines and with dancing. And Miriam sang to them:

'Sing to the Lord, for he has triumphed gloriously; horse and rider he has thrown into the sea.'"
(Ex. 15:20–21)

First Narrator/Preacher: This is Miriam, a dancer, trying to make it in the New York ballet scene. She suffers from bulimia, takes more than the prescribed doses of antidepressants and sleeping pills, is addicted to painkillers she takes for her aching feet and legs, and is considering collagen injections she thinks will improve her looks. She came to New York with high hopes, most of which have faded away. Once ebullient, she is quiet now, looking out at the world from dark, sunken eyes.

> *The young woman looks down. The door opens and then closes. A woman carrying an infant enters, walks to the front and stands next to Miriam.*

Second Narrator:
"Hannah prayed and said,
'My heart exults in the LORD;
my strength is exalted in my God.
My mouth derides my enemies,
    because I rejoice in my victory.'" (1 Sam. 2:1)

First Narrator/Preacher: This is Hannah. She is older than the others in age but not in worldly experience. She married quite young to a decent but dull man. She was lonely and wanted a child. She failed to get pregnant for several years until finally the test strip turned blue. In her ninth month her husband suddenly died, and when her son was born, she was all he had in the world, and he was all she had. A woman with a baby to care for was not exactly in demand by other men in the small town where she lived, so she moved with her son and her younger friends to New York. She got a job in the garment district, but after she paid her share of the expenses, there was little left. She tries to see a brighter future, but that is hard to do.

> *Hannah gently rocks her son Samuel. Once again the door opens and closes. Another woman, slender with swollen belly, enters and walks shyly to the front. She cannot help the smile that graces her face.*

Second Narrator:
"And Mary said,
'My soul magnifies the Lord,
    and my spirit rejoices in God my Savior,
for he has looked with favor on the lowliness of his
    servant.

Surely, from now on all generations will call me
blessed;
for the Mighty One has done great things for me,
and holy is his name'" (Luke 1:46–49).

First Narrator/Preacher: This is Mary, the youngest of our
women. She cannot vote or drive a car—if she had one. She
is unmarried and pregnant. What seemed right went wrong,
and her family was happy when the other women
volunteered to take her with them to New York. She has
no job and earns her keep by cooking and cleaning for the
others. She also baby-sits Samuel and sits looking out the
window a lot. And thinks. In the face of everything, she
remains cheerful and content.

> *Mary wraps her arms around her belly and looks up. The*
> *fourth woman enters, not closing, but slamming the door.*
> *She is dressed in black from boots to turtleneck and wears*
> *her hair long. A guitar is slung over her back. She comes*
> *to the front and paces back and forth in front of the others.*

Second Narrator:
"Then Deborah...sang on that day, saying:
'Hear, O kings; give ear, O princes:
to the LORD I will sing,
I will make melody to the LORD, the God of Israel...
So perish all your enemies, O LORD!
But may your friends be like the sun as it rises in
its might.'" (Judg. 5:1, 3, 31)

First Narrator/Preacher: And last but certainly not least, this
is Deborah, by common consent the leader of the group. A
natural-born leader, Deborah has not only handled all group
negotiations about how and where they would live, she
has also protected the others from harassment and other
trouble. Deborah does not suffer fools gladly, and today
she is angry.

Deborah: I can't believe that judge! If there were ever a clear
case of harassment, this was it. Everybody knows what he
did to her, and the judge threw it out as a "he said—she

said" game. Right. She did say. And the bruises said. And the black eye said. And the broken arm said. And the neighbors said. And the phone records said. How many "saids" does he need?

> *Deborah clinches her fists and turns her back on the audience. Miriam looks up, takes a step forward, and begins to sing:*

Miriam:
Other people have greater dreams;
large is the stage on which they prance.
My dream and stage were small but real;
all I wanted was to dance.
All I asked for was the chance.
My eyes would sting from dripping sweat,
and dust banged up from wooden floor.
But all it ever got for me
were fingers pointed at the door.
"We do not need you any more."
I didn't need to be the star,
praised with money and romance.
Chorus was good enough for me.
All I wanted was to dance...
if they only would have given me the chance.

> *She dances. When the music ends, she returns to her place, and Hannah steps forward.*

Hannah:
Before I moved into this house,
I was a lost and lonely lamb.
I've been alone for most my life;
no one who ever gave a damn,
no one to love me but my Sam.
They tell me not to live through him,
but it's he that has been called, not me.
I know that God has plans for Sam.
Why is it that this frightens me?
Would my God take my Sam from me?
I've no choice but to trust in God;

I'm just a girl from Birmingham.
But I lie sleepless when I think:
not every thicket has a ram
to take the place of my dear Sam.

> *She rocks the child again while stepping back. Mary walks*
> *forward with a quizzical smile on her face.*

Mary:
What's going on with me,
I have no earthly clue.
And maybe that's the point:
what the angel said is true.
I do not understand,
but I love my God so much
that I'm willing to submit
to God's life-giving touch.
And though I am confused
by this gift from God above–
I'm honored to be used
as a vessel of God's love.[11]

> *Mary smiles and backs away. Deborah takes two firm*
> *steps forward, throws up her hands and speaks:*

Deborah: Well, isn't that just precious? What a bunch of "poor
little me" songs! Isn't life hard? Aren't things unfair? Let
go and let God. Well, that and three dollars will get you a
cup of Starbucks. No, when the world strikes out at me, I
strike back! Nobody uses me. Nobody.

When justice dries to a trickle,
and what's right gives way to might;
when they cheat me and abuse me,
they very quickly see the light–
I do not cringe or hide, I fight.
There was a guy who tried to hurt me
When I lived in old St. Jo.
He grabbed me walking in the park,
but there's one thing he did not know:
my belt is black in Tae Kwan Do.

Low pay and ceilings made of glass—
they think they have the right divine
to treat me like I'm second class,
some bimbo chick without a spine.
By God, I'll fight to save what's mine.
I'll fight with everything I have;
I'll fight with all my mind and might.
I will not let them drive me down,
I will not grovel out of sight.
I'll struggle till I die: I'll fight.[12]

> *Deborah shakes her fist as she finishes and stomps back
> to her place.*

Mary: Your songs are all so sad, so hopeless.

Deborah: Hope is for the weak, Mary. The strong don't hope, they act.

Hannah: But if we take action, we'll always lose. They're stronger than we are.

Miriam: Maybe not if we work together.

Deborah: Now you're talking! If we join our songs together, everyone will hear, and they can ignore us no longer.

Other Three: Yes!

Miriam: We'll dance!

Hannah: We'll trust!

Mary: We'll love!

Deborah: We'll FIGHT!

> *Pause.*

Mary: Deborah, it's hard to sing your song.

Deborah: *(shaking her head wistfully)* I'm just doing the best I can in a very hard world.

Mary: *(smiles)* We know.

> *All four embrace in a group hug and then exit.*

First Narrator/Preacher: We've heard the songs of the biblical women. How about our songs? I remember a song we used to sing that goes like this:

"Will the circle be unbroken, by and by, Lord, by and by?

There's a better home a-waitin', in the sky, Lord, in the sky."

I always assumed that was a positive song, an affirmation about the eternal unbroken circle of love that exists among those who love God and one another. But I am beginning to wonder. Could it be, rather, a lamentation? a plea? a petition that God in heaven will finally break the circle of violence and hatred that threatens to destroy us? If that is the case, then break the circle now, O God! Deborah was your friend, scripture says, and yet, trapped by her culture, she could not finally break the circle. What hope then is there for us? A twofold hope. First, the hope that comes when we remember the stories of those, like Deborah, who tried, and we learn from them. Second, when we see that the good news about how God can use all people to accomplish God's work of salvation is good news that drips with blood, another story may come to mind. And then, with the sound of the quartet singing together beside us and the vision of the cross before us, we may in our own time begin to chip away at the circle of hatred, to interrupt the cycle of violence, and to sing with the psalmist a new song before God, a song of peace.[13] O God, help us to be your friends, so that other friends of yours, the Deborahs and Jaels of the future, may be able to study war no more.[14]

Making Good Guesses (Judges 5:10–11)

What is the cause of the violent unrest in so much of the Arab world? The causes are many, some of which may be laid at Western doors. But at least one cause is related to the poverty of so many millions of people while a few sheikhs have become obscenely rich on petrodollars. The injustice inherent in that situation is highly flammable.

Tell of it, you who ride on white donkeys,
  you who sit on rich carpets

and you who walk by the way.
To the sounds of musicians at the watering places,
there they repeat the triumphs of the LORD,
the triumphs of his peasantry in Israel (5:10–11).

There are two reasons I want us to look at this text. The first has to do with the state of the text itself, the second with possible meanings then and now. George Foot Moore, author of the classic International Critical Commentary's volume on Judges, which is still read one hundred years after he wrote it, said this of 5:10–11:

> The text of these verses has suffered so badly that there is no reasonable hope that any art or skill by the critic will ever be able to restore it…It is obviously impossible, as it would be unprofitable, in the obscure and corrupt places of this poem, to discuss or even record all the guesses of commentators.[15]

In the century that has passed since Moore wrote that, no one has really contradicted him. Commentators Robert Boling, Tammi Schneider, and Dennis Olson have all but ignored the text. The conclusion appears to be that we do not know what this text says, much less what it means. Whoever, then, translates this "corrupt" text is guessing.

This result does not rest easily with those who believe scripture to be the "Word of God." One does not like to "guess" at the Word of God. But this is not the only place where we have to do exactly that. When theologians, biblical scholars, and preachers seek to interpret the acts of God for us, they apply both their interpretative skills and faith to the best evidence they can gather and then make the best guesses they can. No theological position is, in its entirety, the last word on the subject. But we must live and die by such less-than-final understandings. We have no other choice this side of the *eschaton.*

According to Moore, all we can really say with any confidence about this text is:

> Men who ride…ruddy asses–that sit on…–and that walk on the road…–from (?) a sound of…between

watering-places—they there rehearse the righteous acts of Yahweh.[16]

Not much to work with although Moore disdained attempts to translate this text, but many others have tried. The NRSV and the NIV have arrived at similar meanings or guesses, which go something like this: The life of the peasantry in Israel prior to Deborah was harsh and cruel. Bandits plagued the countryside, forcing villagers off the roads. But after Deborah's exploits, the people prospered. They traveled the highways on white (or red or tawny or grey—take your pick) donkeys and enjoyed the musicians who had set up shop at the watering-holes to sing praise-choruses to God. Such a picture is a fair guess, I think.

I have a different guess to offer. I sense a gentle rebuke to those now wealthy ones who ride the white donkeys and hang around the watering-holes (translate "bars" or "taverns" perhaps?)[17] praising God. Only a poorly armed remnant joined Deborah and Barak in battle, and I do not think these wealthy ones were among them. I think of the white donkey riders the way Shakespeare has King Henry V think about "gentlemen a-bed in England" prior to the Battle of Agincourt:

We few, we happy few, we band of brothers;
For he to-day that sheds his blood with me
Shall be my brother; be he ne'er so vile,
This day shall gentle his condition:
And gentlemen in England now a-bed
Shall think themselves accursed they were not here,
And hold their manhoods cheap whiles any speaks
That fought with us upon Saint Crispin's day.[18]

Similarly, the point in Deborah's hymn may be that it is the poor who fight and die in war, not the rich. And it is the rich who profit from war, not the poor.[19] That is my guess. What is yours?

Unbearable Choices (Judges 4:17–23; 5:24–27)

When my wife was pregnant twenty-four years ago, we spent many hours pondering names for this child to be. One day we were considering girls' names when I ventured, "How about Jael?"

"What?"

"Jael. An Old Testament heroine who killed the enemy of the Israelites by driving a tent peg into his head. And whether you say 'Yah-El' or 'Jail,' it's a very euphonious sound."

"No."

That ended that. But it did not end my fascination with her story. The story is fertile soil for scholars, but hardpan for preachers. I think this is the most difficult story in Judges to read homiletically. Other stories we can preach or preach against. But this one stymies us. How are we to understand it? And what do we do with it?

We are told that Jael was the wife of Heber the Kenite. The Kenites were allied with the Israelites' enemy, King Jabin. Deborah and Barak fought against Jabin's general Sisera and his army and routed them. Sisera, alone on foot, escaped to Jael's tent. She welcomed him, gave him drink, and then drove a tent peg through his head.

Why? Her action stuns and disorients us. What had she done? She had violated the code of hospitality. She had acted deceitfully. She had murdered one who was not her enemy. And for this the Israelites hailed her, a foreigner no less, as the "most blessed of women"?

We are not the first ones who have had trouble with this text.[20] What is the motivation for Jael's action? Why did she do it? We do not know. The text does not tell us. But that has not kept people from speculating about her motivation. Some say that because it would have been very unusual for a woman to invite a man who was not her husband into her tent, Jael killed Sisera in defense of her honor.[21] Others picture Jael as a kind of protofeminist who, knowing that Sisera is a warrior/ rapist, ensured with a preemptive strike that he would rape no more.[22] Another conjecture is that since the Kenites and Israelites were related through Hobab, the father-in-law of Moses (see Judges 4:11), Jael may have been a secret Yahwist, acting out of covenant loyalty.[23] After all, her name means "Yahweh is God." But the view that makes the most sense to me is the one proposed by Danna Fewell and David Gunn.

This battle of the Kishon took place in the north of Canaan, while the Kenites lived near the Negev in the south. So why were Heber the Kenite and his family so far from home? The Kenites were smiths. Sisera had nine hundred iron chariots. It is not much of a jump to suggest that Heber was in the armaments business, working on Sisera's chariots or other weaponry. The battle was engaged, the Canaanites were routed, and Sisera appeared on foot at Jael's tent. Jael was no fool. She knew that Sisera had lost the battle. She knew that the Israelites would be hot on his trail. And she knew that as allies of Sisera who provided him with military hardware and then hid him from them, her life and the lives of her family would be forfeit. Given this scenario, her only chance to survive was to kill Sisera and present his dead body to Barak. She had no other choice.

Seen in this way, this often condemned story takes on a different look. Many people look to the Bible as a kind of moral answer book. In this situation, do this right thing. In that situation, do that good thing. And that is fine, as far as it goes. But there are some situations in life where there are no good or right answers, where all the available choices are "immoral," where they violate most any code of ethics. This is the choice the father faced in the film *Old Yeller*, when he stole some meat because his children were hungry. This is the choice Bonhoeffer faced in joining the plot to kill Hitler. This is the choice the mother faced in the novel *Sophie's Choice*. With her two children, she is in line before a German officer. He is sending some to the right to work and some to the left to die. When she gets to him, he tells her to choose which of her children will live. She cannot do so. He then motions for both of the children to join the death line, and she has to make an unbearable choice, the worst choice any parent could ever be asked to make. There is no good or right answer.

In a strange way, it is reassuring that the Bible does not duck such real situations. The story of Jael is one. The parable of the unjust steward in Luke 16:1–8 is another. That parable, a real head-scratcher, depicts a steward who saved himself by acting dishonestly and was commended for it. Years ago I asked my teacher what this parable meant, and he said, "It means that sometimes you have to do something." In the thirty years since then, I have not found a better answer. In Dan Via's words, the reader is granted a "moral holiday" in this parable.[24] Strange term. And one that does not work for me. A moral quandary perhaps, but not a holiday. I doubt the steward felt as if he was on holiday. Or Sophie. Or Bonhoeffer. Or the poor father. Or Jael. Rather, they had to do something, and they did it. Barnabas Lindars wrote that "there is no reflection on morals and feelings" in this story. "The moral questions are simply not raised. The story is a story… and nothing more needs to be said."[25] Again, I demur.

The Israelites called Jael the "most blessed of women" for her action because it benefited them. But I doubt Jael reveled in the praise. She was just trying to survive. Few of us will ever face situations that demand choices as unbearable as those of Jael or Sophie or Bonhoeffer. For that we may be grateful. Perhaps there are two morals if not moralisms in the story. One suggests a certain sympathy and concern for those forced to make such decisions. The other encourages us, should such dilemmas befall us, to do the best we can and then, in light of the ethos that surrounds such stories in the Bible, trust the rest to God.

The Mother of Your Enemy (Judges 5:28–30)

Herman Herst, Jr., was the best-known philatelic writer in America for more than half a century. When as a child he told his mother he wanted to be a writer, she said this to him:

> One thing you must remember. Everybody had a mother. The lucky ones still have one. But whenever you write anything, or whenever you give a talk, say something about a mother. It doesn't have to be your mother. It can be anyone's mother. Everyone wants to hear about a mother, because deep down under, this is the first love a person has. If you are talking and the audience is restless, talk about your mother. Put your mother into everything you write. Having had a mother is the one thing in the world that puts every one of us on common ground.[26]

The book of Judges, with its snapshots of wartime existence, anticipates the advice of Hearst's mother by introducing several mother-figures in its stories. But as is so often the case in Judges, the figures are not what we expect. Take, for example, the two mother-figures of chapter 5. Deborah is described as a "mother in Israel," which may be more than an honorific. It may also represent the place and office of a wise woman prophet.[27]

The second mother in the text is Sisera's mother.

"Out of the window she peered,
    the mother of Sisera gazed through the lattice:
'Why is his chariot so long in coming?
    Why tarry the hoofbeats of his chariots?'
Her wisest ladies make answer,
    indeed, she answers the question herself:
'Are they not finding and dividing the spoil?–
    A girl or two for every man;
spoil of dyed stuffs for Sisera,
    spoil of dyed stuffs embroidered,
two pieces of dyed work embroidered for my neck as
    spoil?'" (5:28–30)

The reader has the advantage over Sisera's mother. We know that Sisera is already dead, lying with a tent-peg in his temple. Some want to see an ethical lesson here: plundering an enemy is wrong; abducting women is wrong. But did not the Israelites do the same thing (8:25–26; 21:8–24)? I think rather the story is meant to play on the "good" mother-"bad" mother contrast between Deborah and Sisera's mother.[28] Sisera's mother is made into an object of ridicule, placed in the same gallery with Adonibezek and Eglon. She is caricatured as a type of *zenana* woman, a "kept" woman behind a latticed window, in contrast to the dynamic Deborah. As the wait for her son lengthened, she soothed her anxiety by imagining that Sisera and his men were raping women and gathering plunder as a gift for her,[29] not knowing that her son had already been killed in a kind of "reverse rape."[30] She is thus pictured as a vain, stupid person, comfortable with the way women were treated in her world. Contemporary writer Nehama Aschkenasy is so absorbed with Sisera's mother that she calls her book about women in the Hebrew Bible *Woman at the Window*,[31] and so hostile toward her that she says:

The vicious ancient matron is forever frozen in our cultural memory as the mother who looks through "the lattice," and as a classic example of how the position "at the window" dehumanized women and made them a vehicle of male power, silent collaborators in the intimidation of women.[32]

There are two reasons to decline to participate in such ridicule. First, remember that the narrator has created this scene and put the words in Sisera's mother's mouth. From his vantage point, he (I cannot imagine a woman writing this text) had, of course, no idea what Sisera's mother said or even what kind of person she was. If motives are to be examined, the narrator's should stand trial, not hers. Second, the verse that stops the story for me is 28b:

"Why is his chariot so long in coming?
Why tarry the hoofbeats of his chariot?"

When I pause on these lines, I begin to see not a vain, stupid person, but a mother. I begin to see the millions of mothers down through the years who, sitting by a campfire or standing at the kitchen sink with dishtowel in hand or pacing the widow's walk, have stared into the distance, worrying over their sons and daughters who have gone to war, praying for their safe return. I think of the Paul Laurence Dunbar poem "When Dey 'Listed Colored Soldiers":

Oh, I hugged him, an' I kissed him, an' I baiged him
    not to go;
But he tol' me dat his conscience, hit was callin' to
    him so,
An' he couldn't baih to lingah w'en he had a chanst
    to fight
For de freedom dey had gin him an' de glory of de
    right.
So he kissed me, an' he lef' me, w'en I'd p'omised to
    be true;
An' dey put a knapsack on him, an' a coat all colo'ed
    blue.

So I gin him pap's ol' Bible f'om de bottom of de
   draw',–
W'en dey 'listed colo'ed sojers an' my 'Lias went to
   wah.[33]

I think of the scene early in the film *Saving Private Ryan*
where a Kansas mother who has four sons in combat in World
War II sees a U. S. Army car coming up the road, and she
collapses on her front porch.

I think of all mothers who were the first loves of soldiers
and who have watched and waited for them to come home.
What one sees then is not the evil of Sisera's mother, but the
evil of war.[34] The mother of your enemy is still a mother. Maybe
what we have missed in this text is not her vanity, but something
else. She loved her son.

Is that enough? Unfortunately, no. I cannot completely
rehabilitate Sisera's mother. A story by biblical scholar
Katherine Doob Sakenfeld brings me up short. When she took
her American uneasiness with this story to dialogue with Asian
women, she found a different perspective. Sakenfeld writes:

A group of Korean women were expressing some
enthusiasm for Jael's exploits, and I commented that
most women I knew—white, middle/upper-class North
Americans like me—had trouble with this story... After
a brief pause, there came a bold reply from the far end
of the table, "If you American women would just realize
that your place in this story is with Sisera's mother,
waiting to collect the spoil of your interventions around
the world"...I did not want to hear that.[35]

Alas. As Sakenfeld concludes, it is both disturbing and
profound "to hear the Bible as Word of God through the voices
of those not like myself."[36] Condoning rape and enjoying the
booty of war entail an untenable position that finally will have
its consequences. The next time Sisera's mother and the other
Canaanite women look through the latticed window, the riders
they see will not be Sisera and his troops coming home, but
the Israelites coming for them.

Perhaps the question for us, in light of this story and of the Korean "comfort women" forced into sexual slavery in World War II, and of the reign of rape in the recent Balkan war, is when will this stop? The answer is: only when rape as an instrument of politics and war becomes internationally unacceptable, and violators are punished. And young American women–and men–who listen to violent, hateful, misogynistic music because, as they claim, they like the beat, are not part of the solution. They are part of the problem. They have a thing or two to learn from Deborah, Jael, and Sisera's mother.

CHAPTER 5

Gideon

Judges 6–8

Deborah brought rest to the land. Sin brought trouble. The formula of sin and oppression comes into play again in the Gideon story. Each of the stories that follow this pattern has a twist, and this one is no exception. Israel does what is evil in the sight of the LORD and is given into the hand of Midian. But the judge called forth by God to deliver Israel is not a strong leader in the manner of Othniel, Ehud, Deborah, and Barak. He is, rather, a model of fear. His name is Gideon (also called Jerubba'al). There are no fewer than seven occasions where Gideon's fear is described (6:15, 17, 22, 27, 37, 39 and 7:11).

Some scholars suggest that, based on a structural analysis of the text, the Gideon story is the focal point of the whole book of Judges.[1] Graeme Auld goes further to suggest that

> such a well-connected story must be close to the center of the Old Testament. And the connections are all the more interesting because several of them are not common biblical motifs, but occur only in Judges 6–8 and once or perhaps twice elsewhere.[2]

J. Paul Tanner continues the centering motif by asserting that Gideon's struggle to believe God's promises sits at the center of the Gideon narrative, and that *fear* is at the center of the struggle. No one seems willing to suggest that at the heart of the book of Judges one finds *fear*. It is an interesting possibility. Another suggestion is that, based at the center of the narrative,

Gideon's story represents a significant shift in the "quality" of the judges that served Israel,[3] with Othniel, Ehud, and Deborah to the fore, and with Abimelech, Jephthah, and Samson aft...and lacking.

The story is perhaps more remarkable than its main character. A number of elements of the story lend themselves to the pulpit.[4] Here are a few of them.

He Had It; He Lost It (Judges 6:34, 8:22–28)[5]

Things are looking bad for the Israelites when we arrive at chapter 6 in Judges. The Midianites and the Amalekites and all the people of the East, it says, are massing against the Israelites. And then, 6:34, "The Spirit of the LORD took possession of Gideon; and he sounded the trumpet." That's NRSV. Other translations say the Spirit came upon Gideon or took hold of Gideon. It is an interesting phrase in Hebrew, and there may be an even better translation: "Ruah Yahweh labshah 'eth-Gideon" –"The Spirit of God clothed itself with Gideon."[6]

That's a little different, is it not? Gideon did not put on God; God put on Gideon! Think about it. The initiative and the action are God's. There is an intimacy and power in this Hebrew metaphor that we rarely talk about, but is always true. We see a similar case in *Zohar: The Book of Enlightenment*:

> Come and see:
> The world above and the world below are perfectly balanced:
> Israel below; the angels above.
> Of the angels it is written:
> 'He makes his angels spirits' (Psalm 104:4).
> But when they descend, they put on the garment of this world.
> If they did not put on a garment befitting this world they could not endure in this world
> and the world could not endure them.
> If this is so with the angels, how much more so with Torah.[7]

And how much more so with God? How does God choose to work? Generally not by floating around in the ether, immortal, invisible—but through human hands and personalities. We know this happened with Jesus:

> King of kings yet born of Mary, as of old on earth he
> stood
> Lord of Lords in human vesture, in the body and the
> blood.[8]

But this story about a man named Gideon shows that this is also the way God works with others and wants to work with us. That's the first point. The only chance many people will ever have to experience the spirit of God is as that spirit is clothed with you and me.

I would rather like to stop there. I think it preaches. It is a nice point that hardly anyone could disagree with, and that will get you to the parking lot. Unfortunately, the story goes on. And Gideon's story is the turning point in the book of Judges. From here on, it is all downhill. No pastor interested in church growth will preach about Gideon or God's wanting to downsize the church from 32,000 members to 300. Furthermore, Gideon is a sniveling little guy whose fear requires a continual testing of God.

It often seems that God could do better in choosing God's advocates. Not long ago I said to a gathering of preachers:

> Surely God could have done better than choose us. Well,
> apparently not. There were surely others, better than
> we, that God called. But for some reasons they said no.
> We're the best that God could find, for this time, for
> this place, for these people. Which means, of course,
> that, to go along with God's sense of love and justice,
> God just must have a sense of humor.[9]

God could have been giggling when God got dressed up with Gideon. Pretty poor costume, old sniveling Gideon, but the best God could find on short notice.

And then, with the presence of God palpable in his life, things got better. Gideon became the leader of his people, triumphed over his enemies, and then, when the people asked Gideon to become king and rule over them, he declined, saying "God will rule over you." This is really good. Gideon, who started with nothing but fear, is one inch away from becoming one of the greatest leaders in human history. All he had to do is be faithful to the God who had called him through his remaining years, and his legacy was assured.

But you know the next line, don't you?

> Then Gideon said to them, "Let me make a request of you; each of you give me an earring he has taken as booty"…"We will willingly give them," they answered. So they spread a garment, and each threw into it an earring he had taken as booty. The weight of the golden earrings that he requested was one thousand seven hundred shekels of gold…Gideon made an ephod of it and put it in his town, in Ophrah; and all Israel prostituted themselves to it there, and it became a snare to Gideon and to his family. (8:24–27)

That close. A few earrings. A little idol's covering. And he threw it all away. And people and our book fall apart with him. My colleague Bryan Feille reminded me of the ending of Paddy Chayefsky's play *Gideon.* After the battle was won, the soldiers shouted, "For Gideon and for the Lord!" An angel standing stage left says, "'For Gideon and for the Lord,' indeed. It used to be 'For the Lord and for Gideon.'"[10] And as Gideon puts on his gold ephod, in a perverse switch from God putting on Gideon, the angel says,

> Then let him don my gold ephod
> and let him be a proper god.
> Well, let him try it anyway.
> With this conceit, we end the play.[11]

Downhill. We know stories like this, do we not? People who had it all, people who were richly blessed and then, for some money or a cheap thrill or another idol, threw it all away. Do we think of the good done by television evangelists who have been brought down by scandal? Probably not.

A colleague told me about a minister who was the most dedicated person he had ever met while in seminary. Now he has mansions all over the country. Is that a problem?

Another minister moved his ministry to Dallas, and the first thing he did was to buy a two-million-dollar house for himself. Is that a problem?

I once saw a pastor use the cross on the chain around his neck to clean his fingernails. Is that a problem?

If you saw a preacher that you knew well suddenly show up to preach with a big gold earring like Gideon, a preacher who furthermore didn't know which side symbolized what when wearing an earring, would you have any trouble focusing on the message?[12] Or is who we are and what we do and what we symbolize irrelevant to the message we preach?

The only sermon I have ever read on good beginnings and bad endings was preached a half century ago by Harry Emerson Fosdick. Here's an excerpt:

> There is one character in the New Testament, mentioned only three times, whose name was Demas. First, in Paul's letter to Philemon, we read, "Demas, Luke, my fellow-workers." So Demas, along with Luke, and named first at that, was standing by Paul in his Roman imprisonment, a devoted and promising disciple. Second, in Paul's letter to the Colossians, we read, "Luke, the beloved physician, and Demas." Just Demas. Third, in the Second letter to Timothy, we read, "Demas forsook me, having loved this present age." Three points on a curve, that enable us to plot its graph? For here is the story of a man who made a fine beginning and a poor ending: Demas, my fellow-worker; Demas; Demas forsook me.[13]

I will not comment on the order of Fosdick's texts. But it occurs to me that Demas may be a New Testament parallel to the older story of Gideon: a fine beginning, a disastrous conclusion. So here is the second lesson: keep the faith. After years of taking out the faith and examining it every day, of finding new ways to hold it and look at it, ways of chipping away at it to find out if there really is something underneath, we may descover that the faith can lose its lustre. We do our best, and sometimes it works, and the people cheer, and we say, "Well, could you maybe give me a little earring?" The God who called us will be faithful through the dog days of doubt. Let it not be said of us: "They forsook me."

Now we need to do one more thing. There is a famous story by Albert Outler about Theodosius' horse. The christological controversies were still going strong in the fifth century when Emperor Theodosius finally came out in favor of the Alexandrian position as opposed to the Antiochene one, saying that Christ's divine nature "swallowed up" his human one, thus diminishing the human nature of Christ. However, one day the emperor was out riding, and although he was a good horseman and was well mounted, his horse tripped, and Theodosius was thrown and killed. A new emperor came in who supported Antiochene thought, and the Alexandrians were defeated.[14] It was a little thing, really, a horse stumbling. But if it had not, we might be thinking of Jesus Christ in a very different way today, if we thought of him at all. Historians have told us that Alexandrian theology with its wafty view of Christ would not have been able to withstand the onslaught of Islam in the eighth century, making all of us Muslims today. That would be different, would it not? And all because a horse stumbled.

I once got involved with a similar "what if?" I helped write a story about Wickliffe Campbell, the youngest son of Alexander Campbell, bellwether of the Disciples of Christ.[15] After Alexander's death in 1866, the Disciples entered a dry scholastic period, as no great leader emerged to take Campbell's place. Was there no one with the faith and vision to succeed Campbell? There was one. His son Wickliffe was described as dedicated and brilliant, with the personality necessary to be a religious leader. But it never happened. Wickliffe drowned while swimming in 1847, leading his father to lament Wickliffe as

> a son who gave much promise, and on whom clustered many a hope of future usefulness—greatly devoted to his Bible, pious and most exemplary in his behavior, fond of learning and of books...We had nothing to fear, but everything to hope from him.[16]

My point was that had Wickliffe lived, there was a good chance that he would have succeeded his father in the 1860s and held the fractious Disciples movement together. Some people thought the Wickliffe story fatuous. Now this very procedure has become rather popular. It is called virtual history: the great "what ifs" of history. When it comes to the Bible, people have engaged such alternatives and counterfactuals (they call them) as "What if Judges had been written by a Philistine?" "What if Luke had never met Theophilus?" "What if Paul had gone east instead of west?"[17]

I'll play. What if Judges 8:26 read this way:

> The weight of the golden earrings that he requested was one thousand seven hundred shekels of gold. And Gideon said, "Take this—feed the hungry, clothe the naked, care for the widows and orphans, that we might share the blessings of God with those who need them most."

Would it have made a difference? to Gideon? to the future of the nation? to the book of Judges? I do not know. But would it make a difference if we remained faithful and good stewards of God's blessings? Maybe. And those are better odds than we get with the alternative. Standing with Gideon next to the maelstrom of disintegration and collapse, I remember what Arthur John Gossip said when his life tumbled in, "You in the sunshine may believe the faith, but we in the shadow must believe it. We have nothing else."[18]

Do not throw it away. Keep the faith. In the end we have nothing else.

And there we have it from Gideon of old,
who started with God and ended with gold.
The road we will take is ours to determine,
and with that word we finish this sermon.

"Fleecing" God (Judges 6:36–40)

To read Gideon is to read a fear-driven story. The Deborah story ends with this worshipful praise: "may your friends be like the sun as it rises in its might" (5:31), while the first worship in the Gideon story occurs, in fear, at night (6:27). When God calls on Gideon to deliver Israel, Gideon protests, saying, "My clan is the weakest in Manasseh, and I am the least in my family" (6:15). Sounds like Moses (Ex. 3:7–17) and Isaiah (Isa. 6:5).

Then Gideon asks God for a sign (6:17). Sounds like the scribes and Pharisees before Jesus (Mt. 12:38). Then Gideon whimpers, afraid he will die because he has seen God face to face (6:22). Sounds like Manoah (13:22). Then Gideon is afraid to do the LORD's bidding by day, so he does it by night (6:27). Sounds like Nicodemus (Jn. 3:2). It is as if all the fear in the Bible is gathered up in this character Gideon.

What follows, though, is unique. In the "sign of the fleece" story (6:36–40), Gideon asked God to do one thing. God did. Then Gideon asked God to do the opposite, which God also did. Gideon laid some fleece on the ground and said to God, "If there is dew on the fleece in the morning, but the ground around it is dry, I will believe you when you say that you will deliver Israel by my hand." The next morning, it was so. Was Gideon convinced? No. He said to God, "I'm going to lay the fleece down again and if, in the morning, it is dry and the ground around it wet, I will believe you." The next morning, it was so. Was Gideon convinced? No. The next night the LORD told Gideon to attack the Midianites, but "if you are afraid, go on back to your own camp" (7:9–11). Which Gideon did. Did God ever have a more sniveling champion than Gideon?

Critic David Jobling talks about the importance to meaning of differences and opposites within a text.[19] In this text we notice Gideon is the only judge to whom God speaks directly. Furthermore, no character in Judges receives more divine assurance. And yet no one displays more doubt.[20] I remember an old football coach who said that fear makes cowards of us all. And I wonder if Gideon's chronic fear, in spite of all God's blessings, eventually led him into idolatry.

There may be a two-pronged message for us here. God is persistent in pursuit of us, but our opportunities to respond are not innumerable. We cannot put God to the test *ad infinitum.* Second, God does not always choose the bravest, the best, and brightest to carry out God's mission. That should be good news for all of us.

Why Gideon Is Not the Hero of the Church Growth Movement (Judges 7:2–8)

The story of Gideon's victory over the Midianites is less about the battle than it is about who is to get credit for the victory. Gideon sets forth with 32,000 troops to oppose Midian's 120,000. But God informs Gideon that he has too many soldiers, that when they are victorious, they will take the credit instead of properly ascribing the glory to God. Through two exercises ("Who is not afraid?" and "Who laps water like a dog?"), the army is reduced to 300. God and the 300 lappers are victorious.[21] But Gideon and his soldiers soon forget who gave Midian into their hands. And the world of Israel begins to fall apart.

I have heard this story mentioned only once in church. We were having an elders' meeting on the question of inactive members and what we could do to bring them back into the life of the church. One elder was opposed to putting more "dead wood" back on the active roll. He said with some passion, "Let's *gideonize* this church, get down to fightin' strength, and see what God can do with us." He was outvoted, but I appreciated both his passion and his knowledge of that old biblical story. I also have a friend of whom it has been said that he took a church of 1500 and built it into a church of 300. The rebuilt church *was* more vital, more involved in the life of the community, and better stewards than they had been before. Maybe there is something to this *gideon* thing.

Can you imagine a "church growth" seminar with a sermon on this text, on how to reduce your church from 32,000 to 300 members, so you can give God the glory instead of hoarding it for yourselves? It is an interesting thought. Megachurches do tend to be self-serving, their buildings massive and very expensive, their theology simplistic, their worship entertainingly hopped up with technological wizardry.

While the megachurches get the press and the praise, it remains that the vast majority of churches in this country have fewer than one hundred members. For them this text might be heard as a word of hope, a message that God can indeed do great things with a small and dedicated group of people. Lappers unite!

CHAPTER 6

Abimelech, Disloyalty, and Retribution

Judges 9

If the midpoint of the action and its trajectory in Judges comes with Gideon in chapters 6–8, the precipitous downward spiral begins with Abimelech in chapter 9. The son of Gideon and a secondary wife or *pilegesh* from Shechem, Abimelech seeks the support of the lords of Shechem in his drive toward the throne of Israel. Naomi Steinberg's sociological analysis of the text suggests that Abimelech's problem lay in seeking power through matrilineal kinship rather than the Israelite norm of patrilineal kinship.[1] A related problem is disloyalty. Dennis Olson writes: "The disloyalty and ingratitude that Abimelech and the Shechemites displayed toward their deliverer Gideon is a mirror of the disloyalty and lack of gratitude that Israel as a people showed to the Lord."[2]

Loyalty seems to be a fading part of American life. Time was, people would go to work for a company and spend their entire working lives there, giving their best to the company and expecting the company to take care of them. This is rare today, on both sides. Neither management nor labor seems to feel any loyalty to the other or to the company itself. In fact, the idea of loyalty itself, once deeply ingrained in the culture, tends to strike people as quaint, a remnant of bygone days.

Josiah Royce, a great philosopher from the early part of the twentieth century, went so far as to call his system the "philosophy of loyalty." It is worth taking a moment to see how Royce framed his thinking. Royce began by saying that loyalty had been "a good old popular word, without any exact definition."[3] A preliminary definition might be "the willing and practical and thoroughgoing devotion to a cause."[4] But this posed a problem, because the cause could be good or bad. We do not see, for example, the loyalty that cult members had toward Charles Manson or David Koresh as a good thing. Royce solved this problem by suggesting that a cause is good insofar as it promotes a *loyalty to loyalty*. What did Royce mean by this? In his words:

> A cause is good [when it] is an aid to the furtherance of loyalty in my fellows. It is an evil cause in so far as, despite the loyalty that is arouses in me, it is destructive of loyalty in the world of my fellows.[5]

In my words, when our loyalty to America becomes destructive of other peoples' loyalty to their countries, when our loyalty to Christ becomes destructive of others' loyalty to Buddha or Muhammad, for example, then we have a problem, a problem that can lead to political or religious warfare or both. Royce summed up his position by saying:

> In so far as it lies in your power, so choose your cause and so serve it, that, by reason of your choice and of your service, there shall be more loyalty in the world rather than less.[6]

There is a quaintness to Royce's position, but there is also something compelling about it. Look at the biblical text with loyalty in mind. Did Abimelech bring about an increase in loyalty among the Israelites? No. He hired mercenaries to help him kill his seventy brothers "on one stone" at Ophrah and became the first person in the Bible to assert for himself the title of "king."[7] Jotham, the one son of Gideon to escape the massacre, climbed to the top of Mount Gerizim and told a fable cursing both Abimelech and the Shechemites before running away. Abimelech ruled three years, descending more and more into savagery, until finally he was killed during a siege when a woman dropped a millstone on his head, fatally wounding him. In a futile attempt to avoid the shame of having been killed by a woman, Abimelech had his armor-bearer run him through with a sword.[8] His whole career had been destructive of loyalty, and, after his death, there was nothing left for his soldiers to do but go home. They had no "cause."

Scholars have seen at least three separate traditions gathered in the Abimelech story.[9] But others, such as T. A. Boogaart, see a "unified plot" in the story, one "organized to illustrate dramatically the efficacy of what for Israel was a fundamental principle of reality: retribution."[10] We will see it played out even more dramatically in the Samson story, where Samson said of the Philistines in 15:11: "As they did to me, so I have done to them." The downward spiral of the Judges story is an excellent example of the ineffectiveness of a philosophy of retribution: divine or human. From street gangs to nations, this principle is unfortunately alive and well today. Loyalty has turned into retribution. Israel was the poorer for this, and so are we.

"Mutual Assured Destruction" (Judges 9:7–21, 56–57)

Jotham's fable contains a marvelous story and a barbed conclusion. Jotham, Abimelech's only surviving brother, told the lords of Shechem a story about trees in a forest seeking a king. They offer the throne in turn to the olive tree, the fig tree, and the vine, all of whom turn them down. Finally, the bramble, the most worthless shrub in the forest, accepts their offer and becomes king. The original fable probably ended with the bramble simply saying yes to the invitation, with its meaning or punch found in the irony of the unvalued's ruling over the valued members of forest society. (This would make it very similar to the parable of the sower in Mk 4:3–8 and elsewhere).[11] But Jotham (or the narrator) changed the ending to suit his purpose—that of pronouncing a curse upon *both* Abimelech and Shechem.

At the end of the fable, Jotham said to the Shechemites:

"If, I say, you have acted in good faith and honor with Jerubbaal [Gideon] and with his house this day, then rejoice in Abimelech, and let him also rejoice in you; but if not, let fire come out from Abimelech, and devour the lords of Shechem, and Beth-millo; and let fire come out from the lords of Shechem, and from Beth-millo, and devour Abimelech." (9:19–20)

What fascinates me most about the fable and the whole Abimelech story is the role of the fable according to Graham Ogden. He says:

> Regardless of whatever pre-history the fable may have had or what its form may have been, in its present setting it provides the point of departure for Jotham's pronouncement that Abimelech and his co-conspirators will destroy one another. [The concern added to the fable by Jotham is] that of mutual conflict and destruction.[12]

Does this sound familiar? Consider this description of our nuclear policy during the Cold War:

> Armed with nuclear weapons, the United States and Soviet Union confront each other. Each side feels it must have enough nuclear fire power to deter the other from starting a war. And because of the nuclear threat, neither side wants to start one. The doctrine of Mutual Assured Destruction (MAD) is born.[13]

Actually, mutual assured destruction was born a long time ago. Ask Abimelech and the Shechemites. Now that the Cold War has diminished, how long before MAD returns? Once embarked upon, can MAD ever really be disavowed? By Serbs and Muslims? By Israelis and Palestinians? By Crips and Bloods? By the world's *haves* and *have nots*? Is there any real hope for any of these… apart from God?

"Should I Stop Doing What I Do Best?" (Judges 9:8–13)

In Jotham's fable, as we have seen, the trees went searching for a king. In turn they offer the throne to the olive tree, the fig tree, and the vine. All decline. The olive tree says, "Shall I stop producing my rich oil… and go to sway over the trees?" (9:9) The fig tree says, "Shall I stop producing my sweetness and my delicious fruit?" (9:11) The vine says, "Shall I stop producing my wine?" (9:13) In other words, they all say, "Shall I stop doing what I do best to do something I am not suited for and do not want to do?"

In the twentieth century this problem of Jotham's trees helped to establish the famous Peter Principle, which suggests that in a hierarchy every employee tends to rise to his or her level of incompetence.[14] Many of us have become aware of this principle at work. I am a halfway decent professor; I suspect I would be a lousy dean. This leads us to say that the olive tree, fig tree, and vine were right to decline the woodland throne and to keep doing what they did best.

There's just one problem with this. Because each of the three declined to rule, the throne went to the bramble, the least qualified shrub in the forest. Alas, I have seen this fable used to talk about leadership in the church and the necessity of making wise choices. Again, the problem is that there are no perfect choices for those leadership positions. We decline to serve on the evangelism committee or as elder or as trustee because, we say, there surely must be people in the church better qualified than we are for these positions. But maybe not. Maybe the only one who will accept is the bramble.

The dilemma here requires discernment. It makes sense to say we should find what we do best and then do it. But there are times when the alternatives force us out of our comfort zone for the common good. There may be times when we need the fig tree to say yes.

"They Had No Cause" (Judges 9:55)

The story of Abimelech unraveled, and he descended into madness, slaughtering people for no reason and apparently at random. In yet one more biblical example of "what goes around comes around," Abimelech, who killed his seventy half-brothers on a stone, was ignominiously killed himself.[15] After his death, the text says: "When the Israelites saw that Abimelech was dead, they all went home" (9:55).

A soldier's job is to obey orders, and one of the frequently repeated tragedies of human history has come when military leaders, either madmen or terribly mistaken men, have ordered men into battle for no good reason. At the end of Michael Shaara's powerful novel of the battle of Gettysburg, Generals Robert E. Lee and James Longstreet sit stunned after the disastrous final battle on July 3, 1863. Longstreet finally speaks:

> "I was trying to warn you. But... you have no Cause. You and I, we have no Cause. We have only the army. But if a soldier fights only for soldiers, he cannot ever win. It is only the soldiers who die."[16]

Lee's army would soldier on for almost two more years, but the outcome was effectively decided at Gettysburg. Lee and his surviving soldiers would finally do what one has to do when one has no cause: go home. The Israelites under Abimelech's command had no cause either, and so, when Abimelech died, they went home.

There are causes worth fighting for, worth marching for, going to jail for, dying for. But as I get older, that list narrows. I am no longer willing to stand at the barricades, to go to the wall, for some specious little cause within the church. There is no real loyalty there. So much Christian energy is wasted on matters of little or no consequence. The large issues, such as love and justice, are often neglected while people squabble over hymns and the order of service. Too many of our people, seeing no compelling reason to be part of the faith community, have simply gone home. I pray that history will not look back and judge us, saying, "They had no cause."

CHAPTER 7

Jephthah and His Daughter

Judges 10:6–12:7

The story of Jephthah and his daughter is perhaps the most tragic in all the Bible. One who lacked equal status with his brothers,[1] Jephthah was driven from his home by his own family and then recalled because the tribe needed his military prowess. He fought against foreigners and won; in the end he fought against his own people and won, if you want to call that winning. But in between the two military exploits came the story for which Jephthah is most remembered and despised. His sacrifice of his own daughter in chapter 11 is a tragedy of huge proportions – for his daughter, for Jephthah, for God, for the Israelites, for women, for men, for everyone who has read or heard this text over the past twenty-six hundred years.

In short, as Jephthah prepared to do battle with the Ammonites, the spirit of the LORD came upon him. He then made what has come to be called a rash, foolish, and horrible vow: that should he be victorious, whatever came out of his house to meet him upon his return would be sacrificed as a burnt offering. He was victorious, and his daughter, his only child, came out to meet him with timbrels and dances. Jephthah blamed his daughter for his dilemma: "you have become the cause of great trouble to me...I cannot take back my vow" (11:35). His daughter did not plead for her life, only for a two-month reprieve that she might go and wander on the mountains with her female companions and bewail her virginity. When

"Jephtha's Daughter: A Girl Without a Dream", 1993, by Jason Bronner. Used with permission.

the two months were over, she returned, and he "did with her according to the vow he had made" (11:39).

Down through the centuries, rabbis, Christian scholars, and musicians such as Handel have tried to soften the story, suggesting that the daughter (often given the name Iphigenia) was not killed, but condemned to a life of perpetual virginity. I believe these readers are whistling through the graveyard, since the simplest, most straightforward reading of the text suggests otherwise.

Several questions other than the ones considered in the sermon quoted later in this chapter present themselves. The powerful diptych by Jason Bronner[2] shows Jephthah's daughter on the mountain, surrounded by her sad friends, staring into the distance. Staring back is a young woman from our time. The questions that seem to hang in the air between them are: "Can you help me?" and "Does it get any better?" How do we answer?

Further, the arrival of the spirit of the LORD immediately preceding Jephthah's rash vow is jarring. We believe that the presence of God's spirit with a person is a good thing, a blessing that heightens—or should heighten—one's spiritual and ethical sensitivity. So when the spirit of the LORD comes upon Jephthah, and he immediately does something extremely stupid, we have to wonder. Did Jephthah not see what he did as contrary to life in the spirit? Did Jephthah ignore the spirit? Or was the arrival of the spirit so unimpressive that Jephthah did not know the spirit had come upon him? What does it mean for us to live in the spirit? And why do some people feel the presence of the spirit while others in identical situations do not?[3]

The next question is whether or not this tragedy might have been averted. Jephthah thought not. Others disagree. Three realistic options were available. First, Jephthah's daughter might have persuaded her father not to kill her.[4] Second, the people could have ransomed Jephthah's daughter by countering Jephthah's vow with another vow. In 1 Samuel 14, Saul makes a rash vow, which is countermanded by Jonathan. Saul prepares to kill Jonathan according to his vow, but the people shouted:

"Shall Jonathan die, who has accomplished this great victory in Israel? Far from it! As the LORD lives, not one hair of his head shall fall to the ground; for he has worked with God today." So the people ransomed Jonathan, and he did not die. (Sam. 14:45)[5]

Where were the people when Jephthah's daughter needed them? Where were her friends? Where were those who knew that Jephthah's vow and his plan to carry it out were wrong?

And while we are asking that question, we should not forget to ask: where was the angel of the LORD who intervened in other situations, most especially in the Abraham/Isaac story? The third possibility leads us to ask just where was the ram in the thicket for Jephthah's daughter? Where was the God who rescued Isaac from his father but not the daughter from her father? Nowhere to be found. Jephthah's behavior in this story is execrable. God's is not much better. In an 1865 poem by Charles Heavysege, the poet has Jephthah pray that, as God remembered Abraham and provided a ram for Isaac's redemption, God might also help Jephthah out of his dilemma. He prayed that "her blood thou wilt spare," and asked God in closing "to give me some token that my prayer is heard."

He said, and stood awaiting for the sign,
and hears above the hoarse, bough-bending wind,
the hill-wolf howling on the neighboring height,
and bittern booming in the pool below.[6]

No answer. No ram.

We move from the particulars of the story to the question of how it has been read. Ruth Fox says that the Roman Catholic weekday lectionary compounds the tragedy by following this reading with the response: "Here am I, Lord; I come to do your will" and Psalm 40. She writes:

Does this imply that God approved of Jephthah's impulsive vow or that parents have unlimited, life-threatening authority over their children? Victims of violence should surely never be expected to sing, "Here am I, Lord," on the table of sacrifice.[7]

Another reading that strikes me as almost as horrid as the original vow was shared with me by a colleague. He was present when a student at a fundamentalist seminary, upon hearing the story of Jephthah's daughter, said, "Well, that's what she gets for dancing." The student was not joking.

Against these readings, I would like to stand another contemporary reading. Laurie Feille, a pastor friend, recently returned from a trip to Bosnia. One overwhelming experience after another followed her on her pilgrimage. This was one of them: In Sarajevo, she stood looking at two buildings that stood across a field from each other. A battle had taken place in the space between these buildings. Her church worker guide told the group that a "crazy man" lived in one of the houses. There was an apple tree between the two buildings, and he remembered how much his daughter loved apples. Life was so bleak for the children during the war, he thought. So he timed the Serbs' period of shooting, and when they stopped, he ran into the field and gathered fresh apples. He wanted, in Feille's words, "to give her [his daughter] some sense of the goodness of life while she dodged bullets every day with the rest of the children of Sarajevo."[8] As Feille and the group watched the church worker tell the story, she could tell from the man's face that he was the "crazy man" who had risked his life out of love for his daughter.

It is good, when thinking of Jephthah, who took the life of his daughter, to remember others, such as the "crazy man" of Sarajevo, who risked his own life for his daughter.

Abject Surrender (Judges 10:6–18)

Once again Israel sinned and ran after foreign gods. This time God really got angry: "You have abandoned me and worshiped other gods; therefore I will deliver you no more. Go and cry to the gods whom you have chosen; let them deliver you in the time of your distress" (10:13–14). Then comes an unusual verse. The Israelites said, "We have sinned; do to us whatever seems good to you; but deliver us this day!" (10:15). This strikes the same chord we hear in another text, 1 Samuel 3. When young Samuel, fresh from a theophany, told Eli, the insensitive priest, that the downfall of his house was imminent, Eli said, "It is the LORD; let him do what seems good to him" (1 Sam. 3:18).

What are these lines if not abject surrender? This is not indicative of a loving relationship with God; this is knuckling under to brute force.[9] The point of faith is not to club us into walking the straight and narrow, not for us to capitulate to a blood- and soul-thirsty god. It is not to say, "We have sinned; do to us whatever seems good to you." It is rather to say, "We have sinned against you, O God; forgive us, we pray, and help us to establish a right relationship with you."

When Ostracism Backfires (Judges 11:1–11)

Nobody liked Jephthah. Likely born of Gilead's assignation with a prostitute, as we have seen, he was driven out by his own family, an outcast who became an outlaw. He had only one thing going for him, according to the text: he was a "mighty warrior" (11:1). So when the Ammonites made war against Israel, the elders of Gilead went and begged Jephthah to come back and be their commander. Jephthah's reply is classic: "Are you not the very ones who rejected me and drove me out of my father's house? So why do you come to me now when you are in trouble?" (11:7). The elders gave an evasive answer, but Jephthah returned with them anyway and pursued the course that would lead to victory, glory, and finally disaster.[10]

In Greek history we learn of the process called ostracism, whereby Athenians could banish a public figure. On the appointed day, each voter put a potsherd (*ostrakon*) into an urn marked with the name of the person he wanted ostracized. The person with the most "votes" was then exiled, generally for a term of ten years. Interestingly, a number of exiles, banished in fits of jealousy or prejudice, were recalled because the people realized they needed them.[11]

Similarly, nobody wanted Jephthah until they needed him. Moses and Paul were also black sheep, both involved with murder, until God needed them and met them in a burning bush on Mount Horeb and along the road to Damascus. The United States did not want Lincoln until the country needed him. England did not want Churchill until it needed him. Eisenhower did not want Patton until he needed him. The church did not want Phillips Brooks until it needed him. A surprising number of religious leaders down through history have been outcasts. Luther and Calvin come to mind. Movies such as *The Dirty Dozen* celebrate outcasts recalled and "redeemed" because we need them. I heard a story about a family who stopped going to church because the church had called a woman as pastor. Some months later the family's eldest daughter was involved in a serious accident. The pastor was quickly by their sides and stayed with them throughout the ordeal. They did not want her, you see, until they needed her. When trouble comes, we are quick to seek out the Jephthahs to do our bidding and run our risks. And such action did not end with Jephthah. David Gunn concludes his intertextual study of the Samson story and Isaiah with this provocative line, "as Isaiah might have put it, 'Here am I, send Samson.'"[12]

This is not to say that we should not be wise in our associations with people. It also does not refute the notion that the best predictor of future behavior is past behavior. But it does warn us that judging people by pedigree alone can lead to awkward, even tragic, consequences. Be careful about whom you ostracize. There are two further lessons here, I think, concerning our relationship with God. How much do we miss, how much do we lose, when we seek to relate to God only when we are most in need of God's mercy or love? Moreover, when we feel alone, like outcasts among a people who do not need us, it may be that God needs us in a way we have not imagined, that the gifts God has given us may indeed prove to be useful to God and, in time, to God's people.

"Talitha, Cum" (Judges 11:29–40)[13]

Here is a version of a sermon that has meant a great deal to me. Almost thirty years ago I wrote the one great exegesis paper of my life (everybody should write at least one!). It was the study mentioned in the Introduction of this book, an exegesis of the story of Jephthah's daughter in Judges 11:29–40, and I used what rudimentary skills I had trying to penetrate to the core of the passage. There I found agony and tragedy and horror. And in the thirty years since that time, not a month has gone by in which I have not been haunted by the tragic picture of Jephthah's daughter. Early on I asked, "What kind of God would allow this to happen?" And then I asked, "What kind of man would do this?" And then I asked, "What kind of people would want this in their scripture?" No answers came—just demons. Several times I considered preaching on this text, to exorcise the demons. But I never did, because I had nothing to say.

Two separate events combined to open *my* mouth in this present sermon. I had read two biographies recently, one of Admiral of the Fleet Lord Louis Mountbatten of Burma, and the other of Joseph Goebbels, propaganda minister of the Third Reich.[14] The books are not important to us today, but in both of them are sections of photographs. In the Mountbatten book is a photograph of his favorite cousin, the Grand Duchess Marie, daughter of Czar Nicholas II of Russia.[15] Marie was something very special, and Mountbatten dreamed of marrying her. In the Goebbels biography is a picture of his eldest daughter, Helga, described as an intelligent and precocious child.[16]

And yet, on July 16, 1917, Marie, at the age of eighteen, was dragged into a cellar in Ekaterinburg and shot. Why? Because she was the daughter of the czar. That is why. On April 30, 1945, Helga, at the age of thirteen, was dragged kicking and screaming into a cellar of the Fuehrerbunker in Berlin and murdered with an injection of prussic acid. Why? Because she was the daughter of Goebbels, and her father was afraid of her falling into the hands of the advancing Allies.[17] I sat the two photographs side by side and stared from one to the other. And it was their eyes! They stared back at me and indicted me and begged me to help, and cried out to the world, "I want to live!" As I looked, the photographs of Marie and Helga slowly dissolved into a picture of Jephthah's daughter. And I had to respond. I have to preach about what we have done to our daughters.

It is true that we have not done very well by our sons either. We have sent them out as fodder to be dazed and deafened by cannon roar. We have believed that if we expose them to enough slaughter to numb their human sensibilities, then if they survive, we will have made them *men*. But there is still a difference. At least we gave them a club or a gun and told them to defend themselves. We just told our daughters to die. We just told them to die.

We live in a time when this is beginning to change, but not nearly quickly enough. Scholarship has rediscovered Jephthah's daughter. Phyllis Trible has called upon us to remember and mourn for her:

The daughter of Jephthah lies slain upon the high places.
I weep for you, my little sister.
Very poignant is your story to me;
your courage to me is wonderful,
    surpassing the courage of men.
How are the powerless fallen,
    a terrible sacrifice to a faithless vow![18]

But that is not enough. I have lived with her for too long, and wistful memories are not enough. These memories serve to remind me of the archetypal story from the ancient Mediterranean world of the dancing girl brought before the rulers and, for their entertainment, forced to dance until she dies. It is only in Kazantzakis's retelling of that ancient story that I catch a glimpse of the response I need and must have.

After the dancing girl has finally fallen and died, Odysseus comes and gently picks her up, carries her away, and buries her. Then, on her grave, he raises his cry:

"O small, small dancer with your supple feet...
You served our god and died in his hard service.
May your ten martial toes be blessed forever and ever....
O quivering flame that flickered in the desolate air,
dear sister, we won't let the ravening earth devour you!
You'll perch today on palace roofs like a tall flame
and sweetly sing, a small, small bird with a burning
    plume,
you'll come to herald spring like a swift russet swallow."
He stooped, then planted in the ground an almond pit,
so that one day the harbinger of spring might rise,
the almond tree, and in midwinter, armed with flowers,
drive out the ancient frosthaired nightmare from the
    ground,
that liberty might braid her hair with scented almond
    blossoms.[19]

And so, after her three thousand and my fifty-some years, I testify to you that there is no message we can proclaim, no remembrance we can make, and no offering that we can give to Jephthah's daughter that is acceptable...except resurrection![20]

It has been suggested that Jesus is a type of Isaac, made as Isaac was to carry the wood of his own sacrifice up the hill. But I suggest that Jesus is a type of Jephthah's daughter, a small dancer sacrificed to multiple faithless vows. However, as the song says, "They cut me down, but I leapt up high, for I am the dance that will never, never die."[21] The dance of Jesus goes on. Even now we are preparing to share in that dance of new life on Easter morning. So why cannot the dance of Jephthah's daughter be born again? Why cannot the dance that was once used so tragically to celebrate a military victory be resurrected as a joyful dance of peace?

Another text offers a possibility. The resurrection of Jairus's daughter is one of five passages in the New Testament that preserve the transliterated Aramaic—preserved, in James Sanders's words, as "precious residues" of Jesus and the early church. But the more I look at them, the more I see the whole story writ small in these five expressions:

1. to the daughter who was dead, in Mark 5: *"Talitha cum"* ("Little girl, I say to you, arise.")
2. to the man in Mark 7 who could neither hear nor speak *"Ephphatha"* ("Be opened.")
3. to God in Mark 15: *"Eloi, eloi, lema sabachthani"* ("My God, my God, why have you forsaken me!")
4. from the woman in the garden in John 20: *"Rabbouni"* ("Master!")
5. and from Paul in 1 Corinthians 16: *"Marana tha"* ("Our Lord, come!")

What do we have?

To the woman: "Arise." To the man: "Open your ears and hear. Open your mouth and speak." But did they? Or did they and all the rest forsake him, leaving him to cry to the universe, "Why?" Then, when it was over and too late, the woman finally recognized him and said, "Master!" And the apostle pleaded for all of us, "Jesus, come back, we will do better by you next time."

That was the story two thousand years ago. And except for a few ironic points of sound and light, our men have remained deaf, ears plugged against the sounds of suffering, and silent, tongues cleaved to the roofs of their mouths. Our women have been dehumanized, sent forth to die and stay dead. Will Jesus come back to a deaf and silent and dead world? I do not think so. What would be the point? In the novel called *The Fratricides,* set during the Greek civil war, a priest named Father Yanaros looks out over his warring village on Easter Eve, a village where brother and sister are killing brother and sister, and says with sad conviction, "Christ does not want to be resurrected [here]. He told me so."[22]

Only if our men will hear and speak, only if our women will stand up do we and he and she have a chance. And this is our hope: that remembering is more than just having memories. Remembering at its best is a sacred act that approaches the very threshold of resurrection. For example, when we gather about this table, it will not just be we who gather. Rather, again in James Sanders's words:

> In the celebration of the Holy Communion the whole church is present and the barriers of both time and space have been transcended...Wherever and whenever this celebration takes place the church for that moment is the pilgrim church arriving, just about to step over the threshold...surrounded by "so great a cloud of witnesses."[23]

In remembering Jesus about this table, we not only memorialize his death, we long for his resurrection. And this remembrance and this hope give new life to the whole church, to all the saints. Christ comes to live in us, and through him that great cloud of witnesses comes to us and encounters us and calls us to accountability.

The Mark passage goes even one step farther. "Talitha, cum!" Resurrection in this scene moves subtly out of the province of hope and into the category of commandment. Jesus did not say, "Little girl, I hope you get up." He said, "Get up."

And I choose to take that commandment as universal. Jesus was and is in the "getting-up" business, and as his servants, so must we be. Simply calling to mind and then forgetting Jephthah's daughter and the myriads of others who were cut down before they could flower as persons is no better than calling Jesus to mind and then forgetting him. The true remembrance is the one with staying power.

Therefore, on this day I claim in Christ my portion of the enduring life and work and dance of Jephthah's daughter. And I put your portion of that burden and that possibility upon you that, as Christ lives in us and we in Christ, so she, through us, might live and dance again.

"Little sister, I do not even know your name, but out of your dust blowing in the wind of the Judean desert, I claim your dance.[24] And I call upon your sisters here to rise up and claim their own lives of faith, their own right to walk the jubilee road, their own chance to dance beneath the diamond sky with one hand waving free, their own power to rise up and tear down the bars that surround this table and this pulpit in so many places and under so many systems even to this day."

A few weeks ago a person asked me about a certain seminary. I knew nothing about it, so I went to the library to look at its catalogue. I naturally turned to the field of homiletics. Here is the description of their basic preaching course: "The theory and practice of preaching. Students will prepare, present, and evaluate sermons. Individual attention and evaluation will be provided. For men only."

I would dearly love for this to be the last generation that ever has to put up with that. But with large denominations continuing to bar women from the pulpit, it is not easy to be hopeful. So with my thumb in the dike against the resurgence of fundamentalism, I shout that it is time for the sisters of Jephthah's daughter to minister from the table, to distribute the sacraments of grace and mercy and peace to all God's children. It is time for her sisters to climb into the pulpit to speak a good word for Jesus Christ. And do not be discouraged as you do. Do not be discouraged by ignorance and intransigence or even by goodhearted people who try, but so often say the wrong thing.

Therefore, little boy, beloved man, dear brother, I say to you, "Be opened." Open your ears to the rhythms of your own heart, to the lovely murmurs of the seasons, to the cries of those who suffer and die. And open your mouth. Not to utter faithless vows, but to speak courage to the living and comfort to the dying, to replace the noise of solemn assemblies with a song of the soul. Open your ears and open your mouth and open the road that leads toward tomorrow. There are so many of us, and we are such a lonely crowd. Separately, single-file, we will never make it. And Jesus will never come back. But side by side with our sisters, we have a chance.

Little girl, beloved woman, dear sister, I say to you, "Arise." Get up and get on the road. Drive the ancient frosthaired nightmare out of the ground. Lead us out of this winter of our discontent and into the springtime of faith. I say to you, arise, for the long dark night is over, and it is time for the almond tree to bloom.

Marana tha! With this invocation of the Lord, the sermon ends.

"Shibboleth-Pronouncing" (Judges 12:1–7)

Alexander Procter was an unusual nineteenth-century preacher in western Missouri. He lived and worked during a time when much of frontier religion was trapped in a hidebound literalism. But Procter refused to be so constricted. He read the latest theological books from England and Germany and applied his large mind to the great questions of his time. "His onward-and-upward attitude helped to keep the Disciples of Christ from drowning in a sea of restorationism."[25] As one of his admirers beautifully wrote, "Logic-chopping, hair-splitting, Shibboleth-pronouncing, prejudice-engendering sectarianism, under no guise of pretense or sanctification, had any attraction for him."[26]

My concern here is with the phrase "Shibboleth-pronouncing." Whence does it come? What does it mean? How does it affect us? There is one last story in the Jephthah saga, following his rash vow, his victory over the Ammonites, and his sacrifice of his daughter. In a foretaste of things to come (see chapters 19–21), Jephthah's last battle was not against a foreign nation but against another Israelite tribe, that of Ephraim. The text-given rationale for this civil war makes no sense at all, but fight each other they did.[27] Jephthah and his Gileadites prevailed. Then came this little denouement. After the battle, Jephthah's men protected the Jordan against fugitives from Ephraim. When unknown persons appeared, they were asked if they were Ephraimites. If they said no, they were asked to say "shibboleth." This is a word that meant "flowing stream" or perhaps "ear of grain," but more importantly for the story, it was a word the Ephraimites could not pronounce. The "sh" sound became in their dialect an "s" sound, giving them away. "Sibboleth" pronouncers were then summarily executed. "Shibboleth" was thus a linguistic password used as a test of identity.

This exercise has no doubt been repeated in every conflict since then. I have heard how American troops in Europe during World War II, when confronted by an unknown person who said he was an American, would demand that the stranger say "Which way went the winged whippoorwill," listening to make sure the "w" did not become a German "v."

In religion, shibboleth-pronouncing became a synonym for hewing to a sectarian line and consigning to perdition those who did not. We live in a time when shibboleth-pronouncing has experienced a resurgence in secular and sacred arenas. The retribalization of society, coupled with growing sectarianism among the churches, has forced people to say "shibboleth" if they want to be part of the in-group: the right gang, the right church, the right political party, on the right train to heaven. Yes, we should stand up for what we believe. But we should be very, very careful about condemning those who cannot pronounce their truth claims in exactly the same way we do.

CHAPTER 8

Samson

Judges 13–16

The Samson saga is the best known and remembered of all the stories in Judges. People who have no background in Bible and who could not distinguish Ehud from Johnny B. Goode know about Samson and his exploits. Samson's is a marvelous story crafted by a superb storyteller. Born a Nazirite (consecrated one) to a previously childless couple from the tribe of Dan, Samson grew up to have superhuman strength. The law regulating the behavior of Nazirites in Numbers 6:1–21 says they must not cut their hair, nor drink wine, nor go near a corpse. Samson apparently violated all these proscriptions. He played fast and loose with women and killed Philistines almost as a pastime.[1] Recent scholarship tends to stretch from viewing Samson as a religious hero with tragic elements to an antihero not to be imitated.[2]

The story is good meat for literary critics, but what are preachers to do with it? At what point in the text do we hold up our Bibles and say, "This is the word of God"? Or, perhaps, "This text flies in the face of God's word"? Judges 13–16 may represent the least-preached best-known text in the Bible. One scholar three-quarters of a century ago dismissed the text by saying:

> The story is left to make its own impression. There is no summing up. There is not moralizing. There is no preaching a sermon.[3]

If we examine the story for "preachable" moments, we find that Samson has an unusual birth story that recalls the birth of Isaac and anticipates the birth of Jesus.[4] When Samson becomes a man, he sees a Philistine woman whom he wants to marry, stirring up exogamous concerns. But he marries her anyway, has an untoward experience with her during the wedding festivities, and kills thirty men. He abandons his wife and comes back to her some time later only to find she has been given as a wife to another. This time he angrily commits a "great slaughter" (15:8).

The Philistines ruled over the Israelites at this time, and Samson's raids so intensify the oppression that Judahites, for their own protection, hand him over to the Philistines. But Samson escapes, killing a thousand men this time. In his victory song of 15:16, one modern translator has recaptured the exuberance of both Samson and the storyteller:

With the jawbone of a ruddy ass,
I piled them in a bloody mass![5]

Samson continues to be a thorn in the side of the Philistines. He consorts with a prostitute in Gaza and rips up the city gates. Finally comes his fateful encounter with Delilah, which leads to his capture, his blinding and enslavement, and ultimately, his death. So what's to preach?

The majority of sermons that I can find on this rarely preached story tend to be one of two types. There are sermons that might be called "One Great Thing," because the preachers intended to "Schindlerize" the text, to make Samson into a Deuteronomistic Oskar Schindler, both of them selfish, oversexed dummkopfs who managed under difficult circumstances to do one great thing with their lives and save "Israelites" in the process. But then one has to ask: was what Samson did at the end of his life a great thing? Yes, if you're into vengeance; certainly not, if you happen to be a Philistine. A spin-off of this tack is the Robin Hood approach. Samson is seen as one of God's envoys, fighting the hordes of evil Philistines against enormous odds and, in the end, winning... sort of. Die-hard southerners might see him as a type of Mosby's or Quantrill's Raiders during the War Between the States.

Others twist the text into a "God Answers Prayer" sermon. James Crenshaw summed up his book on Samson by saying that the main point of the story is that "God heeds the cry of those who recognize their own helplessness."[6] But do I really want that? Do I really want a God who is that bloodthirsty and that manipulable by ritual or hairstyle? I think not.

So what is left? I believe the two most compelling and homiletically engaging views are those that see Samson as a mirror of the disintegration of Israel and those that see Samson as a symbol of the tension, theological and personal, between love and vengeance. The first view is represented by Barry Webb, who quotes from Milton's "Samson Agonistes," where a group of Israelites see the bedraggled Samson after his blinding and enslavement, and lament: "O mirror of our fickle state."[7] Webb then writes:

> The story of Samson is the story of Israel recapitulated and focused for us in the life of a single man. As Samson was a "holy" man, Israel was a "holy" nation (Ex. 19:6). As Samson desired to be as other men, Israel desired to be as other nations. As Samson went after foreign women, Israel went after foreign gods. As Samson cried to Yahweh in his extremity and was answered, so did Israel...The Samson story mirrors the story of Israel.[8]

Webb is insistent that the Samson story is "serious," and not one of "comic relief."[9] But the average reader is not convinced whether he or she is looking at a regular mirror or a fun-house mirror that can take a man and make him look like a giant or perhaps a monster.

The second view may be an extrapolation of the first. Dennis Olson contends that Samson's story brings to a climax the intermingled themes of love and vengeance that have been running through the book. He says:

> God strains to reconcile these two poles in the relationship with Israel throughout Judges. On one hand, God proclaims to Israel, "I will never break my covenant with you" (2:1). On the other hand, God threatens to end the relationship and let Israel receive its just

punishment: "You have abandoned me and worshipped other gods; therefore I will deliver you no more." (10:13). Samson embodies these two poles–vengeful retribution and unrelenting love–in his life and relationships. Ultimately, like the two pillars of Dagon's temple (16:30–31), these two opposing poles of vengeance and love will crush Samson and lead to his death.[10]

Both these views come into play in the sermon that follows.

Picturing Samson (Judges 13–16)

I'll say a word. You tell me what you see.
Samson.
Steve Reeves perhaps. Or Placido Domingo. Victor Mature (showing your age with that one). Superman of the Bible. The last judge. Strongest man in the world. Israelite hero. Long hair. Killer of Philistines. Dupe of Delilah. Here is a traditional-type picture, played by operatic tenor Domingo, hair (beautifully)

Placido Domingo as Samson in the opera "Samson et Delila."
Photo by Sara Krullwich/NYT Pictures, used by permission.

grown back, straining at his chains, preparing to destroy the temple of the Philistine God Dagon, again and forever a hero.

A more contemporary picture of Samson might look very different. A team of psychiatrists from the University of California, San Diego, have concluded that Samson exhibited all the symptoms of a serious mental problem called antisocial personality disorder. Their diagnosis, published in the *Archives of General Psychiatry*, bases their finding on readings from Judges 14–16 that show Samson to be a bully, a liar, and a nonconformist who was impulsive, reckless, and cruel to animals.[11] I find this interesting but not particularly compelling. Picturing Samson on a psychiatric couch does not work for me. The ancient judge and the modern psychiatrist are worlds and worldviews apart. It is better to see Samson in his world, asking what functions in our world similarly to how Samson and his story functioned in his world, rather than trying to interpret him through modern categories.

So let us move to another picture. A splendid scholar and writer, J. Cheryl Exum has been studying Samson for more than thirty years, and I suspect she knows more about the Samson text than anyone else. Over the years, Exum has argued at length that "the amoral, witty, libidinous, uncontrollable, destructive, and beneficial Israelite champion is a comic hero, who exhibits many of the contradictions associated with the well-known trickster figure."[12] Of course, literarily speaking, comedy does not always mean funny, and tragedy does not always mean sad. But the Samson story is a comedy for three reasons, she says: (1) it ends on an upbeat rather than a negative note for society[13] ; (2) comedy delights in word play, repetition, burlesque, and hyperbole, especially the ludicrous and ridiculous, which is certainly true of this text; and (3) there is no particular character development.[14] Samson does not learn from his mistakes. He is the same chowderhead at the end that he was at the beginning. And Exum has maintained this position for many years. But recently she widened her viewpoint. Why? Because of some new literary technique, some new exegetical tool? No, not really. She did it because she saw a painting.

Blinded Samson by Lovis Corinth was painted in 1912, one year after Corinth suffered a stroke from which he would never

"Der geblendete Simson", 1912 by Louis Corinth, used by permission.

recover. Is the painting itself a scream against his career cut short? Whatever the impetus, the painting is profoundly unsettling, and Exum writes, "I shall not be able to read the story of Samson ever again without calling to mind Corinth's haunting image of anguish and brokenness."[15] She concludes, "Even if the story is not tragic, the hero is."[16]

My concern here is how something unexpected can change our view of a text, of scripture, of God. Exum understood the text one way for more than thirty years, until one day when she saw a painting. And everything changed. Has the text changed? Or just our way of reading it? When I was in college, I was introduced to the writings of Nikos Kazantzakis and could never look at hope and heaven in quite the same way again. I once heard a man from New Zealand named Ron O'Grady preach on Revelation 4. He said,

"I saw a lamb standing, as though it had been slain."
Dear God! What is happening? We turned to view the lion and instead see this dying lamb.

I don't know how much power this symbolism has to those of you who come from the city. In New Zealand, where I live, we still have a predominantly rural economy. Though our human population is about 3 million, we have a population of over 70 million sheep. You can see who runs the country.

We have grown up with sheep. Each spring, at the lambing season, these fragile, helpless creatures come into the world in their millions. The hill sides are bursting with new-born lambs. And what weak, stupid and helpless animals they are. They are totally dependent. Changes in the weather may mean instant death. Separation from the mother is equally fatal. Orphaned lambs are often hand fed by farmer's children with a baby bottle.

If you are looking for a symbol of all that is weak and helpless you would not find anything better than the tiny, woolly lamb.

How can a lamb possibly be the one who would be able to go to the throne of God and reveal the mystery of life to us all?[17]

And having heard him, I could never read Revelation 4 the same way again. I could go on, and so could you, about experiences, homiletical, artistic, or otherwise that have changed the way we view certain texts and tenets of the faith.

Here then is a picture in words that changed my mind about this text. When John Vannorsdall wrote a thinly-veiled autobiographical story about a retired, depressed seminary president, he named him Samson.[18] Can you see him? He does not look at all like our first three pictures of Samson. Looks more like us, doesn't he? Little old man or little old woman. The first two years of the retirement had gone well, but when the doubts began to come, he was surprised by how easily he yielded to them. He began to wonder if he had ever really trusted in God. He had trusted his competence, his hard work, his accomplishment, but how quickly these passed away, how little they seemed to matter. He realized that nobody called to ask his advice any more; the young faculty he had nurtured no longer needed him; and the secretaries did not even know his name. It had been chiseled not only from his door but from the ethos of the school.

One winter day he was walking in the New England woods when he came to a wall. Having his path blocked seemed to represent the place to which his whole life had come. Vannorsdall says it this way:

> There were two ways to deal with this wall if he wanted to go farther. One was to do what Samson did when he asked God for one more shot at the Philistines. He shook the building until it fell, killing more Philistines than he had formerly killed with the jawbone of an ass. And, it's a fact, Samson is remembered. One route around the wall is to return to the fray, mover and shaker. Show 'em what he can [still] do...
>
> The other possibility was to accept the implications of his own preaching of the gospel. Let it go. To let some things go, at least. Freedom is rooted in part in the trust that God will take the things of our hands and weave them into a future more gracious than the present. Freedom is rooted in the trust that it is ultimately God who lays it to heart that we have been faithful in at least some things. Freedom is rooted in the trust that God touches us gently and for Christ's sake makes harmless our stupidities and other sins. Freedom is rooted in the trust that, whatever our limitation to stop the slaughter in the world, and the starving, the future belongs to God, and that when we have done both our worst and our best, it is God who will create something new, a future woven of both love and justice.[19]

Which way would it be? "Though he had little hair left," Vannorsdall wrote, "he could still take hold of the pillars. Or he could test freedom and trust God. He stood at the wall for a long time."[20]

So do we all. Which way will it be for us? I cannot read about the dilemma of Vannorsdall's Samson without thinking of a story I once heard about a pastor. When retirement came, it did not sit well with him, because he was a doer, the hardest-working pastor one could imagine. So when the chance came for him to start a new church, he jumped at the opportunity. This would be his finest hour. He worked even harder, drew new people and money into the church. Everything was going well. He assumed that when the time came to name a permanent minister for the church, he would be the one. But someone else was chosen, a younger person, a woman. He could not let that go, so he reached for the pillars and pushed as hard as he could. He damaged the church; he damaged the new pastor. But the bricks and boards fell mostly on him. He lost many of his friends and much of the reputation he had built over a lifetime.

I come back to the text now. The NRSV has Samson pray in 16:28: "Lord GOD, remember me and strengthen me only this once, O God, so that with this one act of revenge I may pay back the Philistines for my two eyes." But the Hebrew reads: "so that I may be avenged upon the Philistines for one of my two eyes." Perhaps the translators changed it because it did not make sense to them that someone who has had both of his eyes blinded would seek vengeance for only one eye. Some others say Samson was being humble, not asking for too much, hoping to be avenged for the second eye later on. But I wonder if perhaps Samson was smarter than I have given him credit for. Maybe even in his vengeful mindset, he realized that part of his tragedy, his undoing, was his own fault, that at least one eye's worth of his suffering was his own responsibility. In songster Jimmy Buffett's words, "Some people claim there's a woman to blame. But I know it's my own damn fault."[21] So it was that one eye was avenged by the death of the three thousand Philistines; the other was unavenged unless you consider Samson's act a kind of suicide, revenge upon himself for his own sin.

Samson is at times a comic character. We can laugh at him, but not with him. He is at times a tragic character. We can pity him, as one student said, because in his attempts to find love, he never was loved back. But we should not, as many have done, attempt to make Samson into a type of Christ.[22] Samson is a role model for us in only one thing. When things go wrong, when all our efforts seem to have finally come to naught, and when we stand in the midst of our failure and shout, "If I had my way in this wicked world, I would tear this building down," then before we reach for the pillars, remember Samson. Does God really want this building down, this wall down, this church down, this minister down? As hard as this is for me to say, there are surely times when we need to choke out the words, "God be merciful to me a sinner," turn around, and walk away. Let it go. Let the unavenged eye go and trust God. Some people say that nobody ever loved Samson. But they can't say that nobody ever loved us. Picture finally a man or woman walking away from their anger, walking away and trusting God. It could change everything. End of sermon.

"If the LORD Had Meant to Kill Us" (Judges 13:21–23)

Two of the toughest questions in all the Bible are found in Judges. Let us see them now through the eyes of a response also found in Judges. First, in chapter 6, an angel of the LORD appeared to Gideon and said, "The LORD is with you, you mighty warrior." Gideon answered, "But sir, if the LORD is with us, why then has all this happened to us? And where are all his wonderful deeds that our ancestors recounted to us?" (6:12–13). That is a tough question, one which the angel dodges. We see similar questions in the New Testament. The whole purpose of the book of Revelation was to respond to the question, "How can the Messiah have come, and yet things have not changed?"

The second question is Jephthah's in chapter 11. After having been driven from home as a half-breed by his family, he was recalled when the people needed his military prowess. He said: "Are you not the very ones who rejected me and drove me out of my father's house? So why do you come to me now when you are in trouble?" (11:7). In Psalm 118, the synoptic gospels, Acts, and 1 Peter we find similar thoughts, "The stone that the builders rejected has become the cornerstone."

The most anger- and angst-filled question in human history is perhaps: Why did this happen to me? And seeking an agent, people often translate the question into its theological or social counterparts: Why did God do this to me? Why did you do this to me? There are no easy answers to those questions, as we learn from Job. But a simple response to another fearful outburst in Judges may have something to say on this issue. In chapter 13 an angel visited the wife of Manoah and announced that she was going to have a son. She told her husband of the encounter, and he was present with her for the second theophany, where more instructions were given, and Manoah, who did not know this was an angel of the LORD, suddenly realized just who this visitor was. Manoah then said to his wife, "We shall surely die, for we have seen God" (13:22). Manoah had reason to be frightened. In Exodus 33 Moses was speaking with the LORD when he said, "Show me your glory, I pray" (33:18). The LORD replied, "I will make all my goodness pass before you... but you cannot see my face; for no one shall see me and live" (33:19–20).[23] I remember the time many years ago at a conference when my roommate asked me after dinner: "Would you like to see God?" I knew too little about drugs to understand what he had in mind. But I knew enough about the Bible to decline the opportunity, tempting as it was. The fear of getting too close to God is palpable among us. But Manoah's wife has another approach to this dilemma:

> But his wife said to him, "If the LORD had meant to kill us, he would not have accepted a burnt offering...at our hands, or shown us all these things, or now announced to us such things as these." (Judg. 13:23)

Manoah's wife was and is correct.[24] If God had meant to kill us, God would not have accepted our offerings, would not have shown us all the wonders we have been privileged to see, and would not have told us what marvels await in the future. In other words, one answer to the angry and fearful feeling that we have been steamrolled by God and others is that God has given us a past, a present, and a future. This is a great blessing, especially when we are hurting, when one of our time frames is wounded. Just as parts of the brain learn to compensate for other parts that have been damaged, sometimes the past can take over when the future has careened out of kilter, and the future can override a diseased past. When the future looked bleak, a rabbi gathered his people and said, "You may be the children of dealers in old rags, but you are the grandchildren of prophets, and don't you forget it," taking them back to their heritage, where they could find the courage to stand against the crumbling of their future story. When the past was scrambled by abuse and illness, the preacher reminded her people of the words of Paul in Philippians, "forgetting what lies behind...I press on" (3:13–14), and the words of God in Revelation, "See, I am making all things new" (21:5).

We have a past that is grounded not in the primordial slime, but in the loving creativity of God who made something out of nothing, who flung the stars against the darkness, who made us only a little lower than the angels. And no matter what happens here, we have a future with God who is the Alpha and the Omega of all things and will not cast us as rubbish to the void. Knowing this, we can live with courage and joy in the present. Thanks be to God, who still does not mean to kill us.

The Power and Limits of Blessing (Judges 13:24–25)

"The woman bore a son, and named him Samson. The boy grew, and the LORD blessed him. The spirit of the LORD began to stir him in Mahaneh-dan, between Zorah and Eshtaol." Samson was blessed by God and had God's spirit with him. So what happened? How and why did Samson become such a moral pig?

In his investigation of the relationship between God and human beings in Judges, Richard Bowman concludes that "the presence of God with the human leader or the leader's possession by the spirit of the Lord does not guarantee success. Divine success appears contingent upon an appropriate human response."[25] And Samson's was hardly appropriate.

All of us know persons who appeared to be richly blessed with strength of mind, body, and spirit, and yet who, for reasons known or unknown, spoiled their blessing and ended up broken and bitter. Preachers are not exempt. Fred Craddock has vividly warned us of the narrow line between trusting the Spirit in our preaching and falling into sloth:

> All of us know it is God who wakens the ear and loosens the tongue. Having expressed that conviction, it is

important to say clearly that, on the practical level, the task of preaching cannot be divided into the Spirit's work and our work. That is, believing in the Spirit does not cut our work in half. God's activity in the world does not reduce ours one iota. Any doctrine of the Holy Spirit that relieves me of my work and responsibility is plainly false.[26]

Not only does blessing require a human response, it is no guarantee of an easy life – in the Bible, in our lives. A blessing does what it says; it blesses. And to be blessed is to find favor with God. Jesus also was blessed. He grew in favor with God and humankind, and his life was not easy. In one of the most powerful sermons I've ever heard, a young woman put a scarf around her head and became Mary, the mother of Jesus. "Hail, Mary," she heard the voice, "Blessed art thou among women." She was blessed. And then she told us her story, what it was like in that culture to be unmarried and pregnant, to have a child you loved but could not *understand*, and eventually to have to *stand under* him and look up at him, nailed to a Roman cross. Blessed was she. As she left, concluding the sermon, she turned, remembering, and said, "Oh yes, my friends, may God bless you." *Kyrie eleison!*

To find favor with God does not equal chirpy optimism. Bless is not bliss. But it is ultimately the best news of all, because it means that in and out of season, in the best and worst of times, God is with us… again and again. Did Samson know that? I do not know. But I know that we have now been blessed by one crucified, risen, and coming again. The blessings that we do, that we are for one another, foreshadow his coming again in all his glory.[27]

Prescription for a Bad Marriage—and Perhaps a Bad Faith (Judges 14:1–15:8)

By the time we reach Samson's birth and youth at the end of chapter 13, we are prepared for him to assume his role as hero and deliverer. Chapter 14 disabuses us of that in a hurry. Samson sees a Philistine woman in the town of Timnah, and then, without even talking with her, commands his parents to "get her for me." When they ask why he cannot choose a wife from among his own people, he replies (v. 3, NRSV) "because she pleases me." The literal rendering is more telling: "because she is the right one in my eyes."[28] This is an unusual way of describing a woman's appearance, suggesting that something else may be going on. Could this be another in a series of "doing what is right in one's own eyes instead of God's" that leads to the utter calamities of chapters 19–21, a way station on the road to disaster? The wedding celebration, the marriage, and everything after that go terribly wrong. Lust, envy, bitterness, and violent vengeance highlight the marriage of Samson. The way he puts his wife in an impossible position, one that would get her killed, foreshadows the tragic story of the Levite's wife.

When we read biblical stories about cultural phenomena, such as marriage, we must be careful about translating their conclusions directly into our twenty-first-century world. Some want to make such direct translations. Samson's story should be sufficient warning not to do so. It is no model for courtship and marriage. It may well be a model for the disaster that attends self-centered decision-making, ignoring God and making one's own whims the basis for living. In the signature paragraph from Zora Neale Hurston's magnificent novel of African American life in the southern United States, *Their Eyes Were Watching God*, a group of folk were huddled in a shanty at night waiting out a massive hurricane.

> The wind came back with triple fury, and put out the light for the last time. They sat in company with the others in other shanties, their eyes straining against crude walls and their souls asking if He meant to measure their puny might against His. They seemed to be staring at the dark, but their eyes were watching God.[29]

Samson's eyes were not. So few today are.

Asking for Help (Judges 14:3; 16:26)

A woman had gone to a psychiatrist for help with her depression and violent mood swings. After she spoke for a brief time, the doctor said, "Let me describe what I hear you saying," and then told her what her life had been like, as if he had known her for years instead of a few minutes. She was amazed. Then he asked if there were any members of her family who had had trouble with this and, suddenly, for the first time, she saw clearly how her father had struggled all his life against depression. But he had never once sought help for this because it just was not done then. Like so many others, he had just toughed it out.

Psychotherapist Sheldon Kopp writes about the same thing from a slightly different perspective: his own. Kopp developed brain cancer and underwent serious brain surgery that almost killed him and left him partially deaf and psychotic. He slowly recovered and then fell into a deep depression. So he went to see an older therapist whom he trusted. Writing about the session, Kopp said:

> The day I went to his office, I felt frightened, but was grimly determined to work things out. I told him my story in a detailed and well-organized account, and stated that I wanted to get to work right away, to get past this depression, to get back on my feet. Though sympathetic to the pain of my ordeal, his wry answer to my impatience was: "How come a big tough guy like you is thrown by a little thing like a brain tumor?" [He] turned me around in a way that helped me to laugh at myself for thinking that I should be able to handle anything, without sorrow, rest, or comfort.[30]

Coming to Samson's defense in light of his amorality and murderous rampages is not easy. One approach has been to claim that although his appetites were often self-centered, he did not press others to do his bidding. He did everything on his own. He never asked the smallest service for himself, the rabbis noted. And one put the following words in Samson's mouth during his last prayer: "Master of the universe, remember on my behalf the twenty-two years I judged Israel and never presumed to say to anyone, 'Carry my staff from here to there.'"[31] There is no indication in the text that Samson ever laughed at himself, no suggestion that anyone ever asked Samson why a big tough guy like him was thrown by little things like betrayal, blindness, and slavery.

This is a bit of a problem, since the first and last words he is credited with having said to people were requests for help. To his father the young Samson said of a woman, "Get her for me" (14:3). To his young attendant who led the blind man around on the last day of his life, he said, "Let me feel the pillars on which the house rests" (16:26). But these were requests for help motivated by lust and vengeance, not a desire for either self-improvement or more effective leadership. And that is the crux of the matter.

I have said earlier that the book of Judges is, more than any other thing, about leadership. And here in the story of Samson, the last judge of Israel, we find not one single picture of Samson in a leadership role. Leaders are often measured by the quality of people they gather to help them. Everything Samson did was done for himself and not for others. "Unlike his predecessor Deborah, Samson showed no ability to build coalitions and share power."[32] Samson attracted no one to help him. Every action of his was taken alone. His own people were afraid of him and gave him over to the Philistines. In the story of the decline and fall of Samson, Judges says to the people of Israel and to us, "Beware of leaders who never ask for help."

Samson the Terrorist? (Judges 15:1–8)

Samson was a terrorist.[33] At least he was if you were a Philistine. We talk as if terrorism were a new phenomenon. It is not new. It is as it always has been: the strategy of the weak against the strong, the few against the many, the powerless against the powerful. The ironic difference in this text is that the representative of the weaker people—in this case, the Hebrews—is the strongest man of all, at least for a while.

In chapter 14 of Judges, as we have seen, Samson takes a wife from among the Philistines, immediately gets into a dispute with the Philistines, and in "hot anger" [read "road rage"?] kills thirty men and leaves, abandoning his new wife. In chapter 15 he returns to fetch her, but finds that she has been given to another, either because her father thought Samson had rejected her [so reads the text], or perhaps as a not very subtle form of payback. Samson's retort, "This time, when I do mischief to the Philistines, I will be without blame" (15:3), sets the stage for his next violent act, tying torches to the tails of foxes and setting them loose in the Philistines' fields of grain, burning all their fields and vineyards and olive groves.

The Philistines reply by burning Samson's wife and father-in-law. Samson thereupon makes this rejoinder: "If this is what you do, I swear I will not stop until I have taken revenge on you." He then "struck them down hip and thigh with great slaughter" (vv. 7–8). Later he is captured, but escapes and kills a thousand more men with the jawbone of an ass. With the help of Delilah the Philistines shear Samson of his strength and blind him. In a final act of retribution, after his hair has grown out, Samson pulls down the temple of Dagon upon the celebrating Philistines, killing three thousand [can we say innocent?] men and women, while committing a ritual act of suicide that has become familiar to us in these days. The whole story is one retributive act of vengeance after another. And if there is any point here, perhaps it is this: none of them work.

The destruction of the World Trade Center, the devastation of the Pentagon, and the deaths of so many thousands have left us distraught and angry. The Samson-like call for revenge and slaughter has been sounded again. Will it work? Probably not. If we were to ferret out and eliminate every person even remotely responsible for these heinous acts, there will remain one hundred thousand ten-year-olds out there somewhere waiting for their chance to destroy America.

The short-term response to these acts may well be violent and bloody. And as Samson himself might say, we would feel ourselves to be "without blame." The long-term response may have to be a change in the way we relate to much of the world.

Two Roads that Lead to Peace…and One that Does Not (Judges 15:11)

In the Joseph saga (Genesis 37–45), we find stories about two different roads to peace.[34] The first is personified by Reuben. After Joseph's brothers get tired of his proud ways, they decide to kill him. But his elder brother Reuben steps up and says to shed no blood, to throw him in the pit if necessary, but not to kill him (37:21–22). This was not shalom; no harmony was gained. But at least Joseph was not killed. Reuben chose a lesser evil, took a negative road to peace if you will. His act exemplified the negative of the golden rule with which we are so familiar. The negative rule, "That which you do not want others to do to you, do not do to them" is the oldest rule of religion, thousands of years older than its positive version, and still valuable.

Several chapters later, after Joseph–sold into slavery–has risen to become the number two man in all of Egypt, his remaining brothers come twice to Egypt seeking food because of a drought in Canaan. Joseph, though trickery, makes it appear that Benjamin, the youngest brother, is a thief. This time it is Judah who steps up. Not knowing he is speaking to Joseph, he recounts what they did to their brother Joseph years ago, how it had affected Jacob their father, and how the loss of his youngest child, Benjamin, would be more of a burden than he could bear. Judah then steps forward and offers to be Joseph's slave if he will let Benjamin go (44:33).

These two roads, one of not doing to others what you do not want them to do to you, and the other of being willing to offer yourself up on the altar of peace, remain keys to the attainment of peace in our time. The Samson story, alas, gives us a vivid example of a road that did not, does not, and will never lead to peace. After Samson had struck down the Philistines "with great slaughter" (15:8), his own Judahite people said to him, "Do you not know that the Philistines are rulers over us? What then have you done to us?" "Us," you notice, not "them." The Judahites know who will pay for Samson's escapades. They will. Samson shrugs and says, "As they did to me, so have I done to them."

That is a perversion of the ancient rule that is the basis for civilization and religion. It is also the enemy of peace. With Samson's attitude, there is no hope for peace between Philistines and Judahites in Canaan, between Serbs and Muslims in Bosnia, between Catholics and Protestants in Northern Ireland, between Crips and Bloods in the 'hood. As this is being written, President Bush is preparing to send nominees for the federal bench to the Senate. Republicans in the Senate rejected scores of President Clinton's nominees, many without a hearing. Democrats are now champing at the bit for payback. "As they did to us, so will we do to them." Both sides are playing Samson's game. Eventually, both sides—and the country—will lose. Ask Samson.

Delilah and Jael (Judges 16:1–21)

Jael, whom we have seen earlier in chapters 4 and 5, welcomed an enemy of the Israelites into her dwelling, deceived him about her intentions, lulled him to sleep, and then killed him. For this she was considered "most blessed of women" (5:24). A few stories later in Judges, Delilah welcomes an enemy of the Philistines into her dwelling,[35] deceives him about her intentions, lulls him to sleep, and then betrays him, precipitating his death. For this she has been labeled by history as a treacherous temptress who betrays her lover for money. Once more we see the importance of the person who writes the texts. One writer's hero is another's traitor. If Judges were a Canaanite/Philistine text, it would of course read very differently.[36]

There are at least two other things to consider. First, I have no illusions that in the patriarchal society of ancient Israel women wrote the biblical texts. But some texts bear a woman's touch if not her pen-work.[37] The Jael story may well be one of these. After all, the text reminds us that Yahweh was to give the enemy into the hand of a woman. The Samson saga, on the other hand, is a male story through and through. All his encounters with women are laden with sexual innuendo, not relationship. And Delilah's role as temptress and betrayer falls into line with similarly—and often unfairly—typecast women from Eve to Mata Hari. So gender needs to be considered along with ethnicity when pondering the sources of texts.

In the earlier section on "Unbearable Choices," I suggested a motive for Jael's action: the survival of her family and herself. What might we say about Delilah's motive? The two most common answers are patriotism (if Delilah was a Philistine) and money. While both of these are possible, there is another suggestion, one that moves Delilah beyond the realm of gold-digging femme fatale and one that I find plausible. A large amount of material, chapters 14 and 15, are given over to Samson's ill-fated marriage to a Philistine woman from Timnah.

Because of her unchosen association with Samson and through no fault of her own, the woman was burned by her own people. And, as Mary Cartledge-Hayes asks, "What if Delilah knew of Samson's exploits in Timnah?"[38]

> If Delilah knew of Samson's failed marriage and the horrible events that led to his wife's death, then her actions would be explainable not only as patriotic but also as retributive justice.[39]

Finally, I once preached a sermon about two other biblical women: Ruth and Esther. My point was that Ruth rejected her ethnicity to go with Naomi, while Esther claimed her ethnicity as the prime datum of her life.[40] One woman suggested that I may have missed an important point. Their decisions were not governed by ethnicity, but by gender. Ruth and Esther were two women trying to survive under difficult circumstances in a very patriarchal world. Could the same thing be said of Jael and Delilah? Probably. Jael, by her act, saved herself and her family. Claudia V. Camp writes, that at the end of the Samson story "only God, and perhaps Delilah, remains."[41]

The Hair on His Head Began to Grow (Judges 16:22)

"I'm sorry," the doctor said. "You have cancer." That news hurled the young woman into a maelstrom of pain, fear, and confusion. Colleen began chemotherapy and soon began to look like an anorexic waif with dark circles under her eyes. And then her hair fell out. In clumps. Until she was bald as an egg. Colleen struggled on–against the cancer, against the depression. And then, finally one day, the tide began to turn in her favor. Slowly at first. Her strength was returning. Her cancer markers were dropping. And the sign or symbol of that turn was this: the hair on her head began to grow.

The teenager had been drinking. He knew better. Got in his car anyway. Did not fasten the seat belt. How many more dumb things could he do? One. Ran a red light. The accident threw Richard through the windshield, slicing his scalp. Two weeks in a coma. Three surgeries, two skin grafts. Then, finally, the hair on his head began to grow. And with it grew hope.

Of all the candidates for key line in the Samson story, I vote for this one: "the hair on his head began to grow." If in fact the Samson story is a mirror of the disintegration of early Israel, it also is not without hope. I see "the hair on his head began to grow" as the literary equivalent of the prophetic "If my people will turn from their wicked ways, I will forgive their sin and heal their land." Things are indeed bad, but they are not without hope. There lies within the line the hope that God's relationship with Samson, that is to say Israel, can be restored. Tammi J. Schneider writes,

> Samson claimed the source of his strength was his hair when it was the Israelite deity: the symbol of the bond between them was Samson's hair. When Samson's hair was cut, so too was the bond and the deity was no longer with him. This functions, to a large extent, as a metaphor of Israel and her deity's relationship. Throughout the book the deity tried to maintain the bond while Israel slowly snipped away the threads of that bond.[42]

Does this not show the importance of symbols: hair, cross, table? And also that the real power lay not in the symbol but in the God who was behind it? When the hair begins to grow, when the cross is raised to the steeple of the bombed-out but rebuilt church, we realize that the foibles and evil that have separated us from God are not forever, that God reaches out in love again and again in the hope that we will respond. Samson's response was, alas, in character, and the result was death: his and so many others. Perhaps we can learn and change.

CHAPTER 9

Micah and the Danites

Judges 17–18

In Judges 17 and 18 two stories merge into one of the most unusual tales in the whole book. A man named Micah stole money from his mother, returned it, and was forgiven by his mother, who then had an idol cast from part of the silver. Micah put the idol in a shrine with other accoutrements and installed his son as priest. Then an unemployed Levite from Bethlehem arrived, looking for work, and Micah replaced his son with the Levite.

The migrating tribe of Dan soon arrived at Micah's, and took his idol and his priest. Micah protested, but was powerless to stop them.[1] The Danites then destroyed the city and people of Laish and built their own city in its place.

Until recently scholars believed chapters 17–21 were a later addition to Judges for several reasons: (1) the formula (sin, cry, deliverance, peace) disappears, (2) no judges, (3) no external enemies, and (4) no heroic action.[2] But some now see 17–21 as completing a frame with 1:1–3:6.

A. First Prologue (1:1–2:5): Land occupation is dependent on cultic loyalty.

B. Second Prologue (2:6–3:6): Failure to occupy the land promotes cultic disloyalty.

B'. First Denouement (17:1–18:31): Failure to occupy the land promotes cultic disloyalty.

A'. Second Denouement (19:1–21:25): Failure of cultic loyalty promotes covenant injustice.

This chiastic model suggests that 17–18 and 2:6–3:6 are designed to frame symmetrically Judges' main body of deliverer stories.[3] Among the correspondences: (1) Israel's multigenerational degeneration into idolatry (2:10, 17, 19) and Micah's inducement to idolatry by his mother (17:1–6); (2) concern to test Israel's cultic loyalty to the LORD as prescribed by Moses (2:12–3:4) and the aberration from cultic loyalty to the LORD by Moses' own descendant (17:7–12; 18:2b-6, 18–20, 30); and (3) Israel's national apostasy from the LORD's cult (2:11–13, 19) and Dan's tribal apostasy from the LORD's cult (18:14–26, 30a, 31).

I find this persuasive enough to accept at least the idea that 17–21 are more than a tacked-on afterthought to 1–16, but rather part of a clever and well-written frame to the story of Israel's religious disintegration and, in Schneider's words, one which provides "a perfect bridge from the previous stories…to the major catastrophe at the end."[4]

The internal structure of these texts is also interesting. Judges 17–18 and 19–21 seem to share a similar pattern. Both move from individual to tribal concerns. There is smaller-scale patterning in 17–18. Judges 17:1–6 and 7–13 have similar patterns. Both begin "There was a man" and both end with additions made to Micah's shrine.[5]

There is repetition. Three times in chapter 18 we are reminded that the cult objects in the Danite shrine are human-made and thus false.[6] And the main formula (A) of Judges: "Once again the Israelites did what was evil in the sight of the Lord," is replaced by a new formula (B), "Everyone did what was right in their own eyes" (17:6, 21:25; short version in 18:1 and 19:1). Both A and B address idolatry. In A idolatry is seen as that which is evil in God's eyes; in B as that which is right in the eyes of the Israelites. In other words,

> While Yahweh views idolatry as objectionable, the Israelites see it as an acceptable practice. Hence the incorrigibility of idolatry…The power of idolatry consists of the strange fact that God's people regarded

idolatry as a legitimate expression of their worship of Yahweh.[7]

We are reminded several times that "there was no king in Israel." The argument over whether Judges is pro- or anti-monarchical has been inconclusive. One of the things that has surprised me in my research is that most of the recent work on Judges has been done by two groups: feminists and conservatives. The liberal academic establishment is largely absent. Most of the articles that I wanted I had to find elsewhere, because the library where I work does not carry many of the conservative journals. I assume feminists are here en masse because of the sheer number of women and women's stories in Judges and because the stories range from glorious to horrific. I believe conservatives are here because they see a text that supports "true" religion and gives them a chance to lift up Christ the King. I was not a lectionary preacher when I was a pastor and so never celebrated Christ the King Sunday. After working with this text, I don't think I would want to do so. The Hebrew Bible teaches us, it seems to me, how strong is our desire for a king and, in the end, how foolish. I am not in favor of a monarchy, but I think I would rather have that than a theocracy or a christocracy, with all the variety of people who would be telling us exactly what that meant.

Several interesting questions are in 17–18. Why is Micah's name written two different ways in Hebrew: Michah in 17:5, 9, 12 and 13 and Michayahu in 17:1 and 4?[8] Is Micah's mother Delilah? Remember the 1100 pieces of silver Delilah received for betraying Samson. Is that the same 1100 pieces of silver Micah steals from his mother?[9] Is the Levite the grandson of Moses literally or figuratively? Why the emphasis on the Danites, a minor half-caste tribe? Could it be because Samson was a Danite? That would make Micah's loss to the Danites supremely ironic. We shall never know the answer to these questions, but they do increase our curiosity about the relationship between this unusual story and the rest of the book.

What, then, is the point of this story? The narrator, in depicting the main actors of 17–18, gives us a clue by exhibiting a "mild contempt" toward all of them.[10] Depending on perspective, there are several themes. Wrong worship and bad ministry head my list, and I shall have more to say about these in the vignettes that follow. Three other issues raised by this text are unholy conquest, religious hostility, and the need (or not) for a king.

Twice the people of Laish are described as "quiet and unsuspecting." The key term, usually translated "quiet" or "peaceful" is "the same term used previously at four important junctures in the book of Judges to describe the 'rest' for the land that is secured by God's work through a judge."[11] The Danites destroyed that rest, an indication that their conquest certainly did not have God's approval. Some argue that the point of the text is to debunk the shrine of Dan.[12] Others suggest a hidden polemic against Beth-El in favor of Shiloh.[13] Even then, apparently, religious centers (read denominations) did not get along. Finally, scholars have argued for a long time about whether chapters 17–18 are arguing for or against a king.[14] Gale Yee's ideological interpretation suggests the text is arguing in favor of Josiah's reforms and against the old familial economy.[15] In writing about chapters 17–18, John Hercus said that he had "never heard a single reference from pulpit or song writer or study or anyone else at all" about these two chapters.[16] But I find these two chapters loaded with homiletical possibilities.

Wrong Worship (Judges 17:1–6; 18:18–20, 31)

In the book of Genesis we read:

> In the course of time Cain brought to the LORD an offering of the fruit of the ground, and Abel for his part brought of the firstlings of his flock, their fat portions. And the LORD had regard for Abel and his offering, but for Cain and his offering he had no regard (4:3–5).

Thus was the first worship service in our history a failure and a warning. Worship is dangerous stuff. Be careful. There are no guarantees that God will be pleased by ritual acts. As God says to a sinful people in the book of Isaiah: "When you stretch out your hands, I will hide my eyes from you; even though you make many prayers, I will not listen" (1:15). Another strong warning against failure in worship comes in Judges 17–18. Everything in both chapters reinforces the author's depiction of worship gone wrong. For example, an idol became the focal point of both private and tribal worship, and not just an idol, but one made of money, and not just of money, but of "cursed" money. The central character in the story, Micah, also added other illegitimate worship objects, *ephod* and *teraphim,* and an illegitimate priest, his son, to his worship center. Then Micah fired his son and hired a Levite, equating having an upscale priest with increased blessing from God. And finally, the Danites built their shrine with a stolen idol and hireling priest, compounding the idolatry.

Idolatry in our own time is more subtle and perhaps even more invidious. Few people set up shrines to Baal or Chemosh, but many set up shrines to themselves, tended by the spirits of money, sex, and power. The text argues strongly against religious syncretism, against lowest-common-denominator religion, against trying to make the sacred secular and the secular sacred. Some time ago I heard about a new minister in a local church. He is called the Minister of Sports, and he is building a forty-seven team athletic program to be based on twenty baseball and softball fields, nine soccer fields, six football fields, and four tennis courts on more than eighty acres of land. He is also building a $5 million, 56,000-square-foot sports and fitness center with volleyball courts, a hockey rink, and a climbing wall. "It is a place," he is reported to have said, "where people can get in shape and get saved at the same time." In the face of this "new wave of ministry" I think of those little groups of people who gather every week in joy and sometimes sorrow, not to hear some grandiose scheme to cozy up to the culture, but to hear a promise, a promise that comes when they hear the words, "Fear not, little flock, for it is God's good pleasure to give you the kingdom" (adapted from Luke 12:32).[17]

Bad Ministry (Judges 17:7–13, 18:18–20)

Many, perhaps most, of my best friends are ministers. Most of them work harder than people know, and many of them get psychologically beat up on a regular basis by unkind people. Nevertheless, some ministers out there merit the criticism they get. There are two literary pieces that I believe all ministers should read every time they are thinking of relocating and at least once a year. The first is a piece from John Milton's "Lycidas," called by many the finest short poem in the English language.

During Milton's time the Anglican clergy had reached its nadir and was fouled in corruption and uselessness. Milton's hope rested in a brilliant and dedicated young friend and clergyman named Edward King. But King died when a storm took the ship in which he was traveling on the Irish Sea. Milton, devastated, wrote the "Lycidas" as both a lament for King and a condemnation of the languid clergy. In this section, St. Peter speaks:

> How well could I have spared for thee, young swain,
> enow of such as, for their bellies' sake,
> creep, and intrude, and climb into the fold!
> Of other care they little reckoning make
> than how to scramble at the shearers' feast,
> and shove away the worthy bidden guest.
> Blind mouths! That scarce themselves know how to hold
> a sheep-hook, or have learned aught else the least
> that to the faithful herdman's art belongs!
> What recks it them? What need they? They are sped;
> and, when they list, their lean and flashy songs
> grate on their scrannel pipes of wretched straw;
> the hungry sheep look up, and are not fed.[18]

If there is the slightest possibility that Milton writes also of us, we must repent immediately.

The second rebuke comes from the classic story of the hireling priest in Judges 17–18. He is first described not as one responding to a call, but rather as one simply looking for a job. Furthermore, as a Levite, he had to have understood the illegitimacy and the idolatry involved in the position he accepted. He compounds his apostasy by selling out to the Danites for a more "prestigious" position. His is clearly a ministry for sale to the highest bidder. Then, when called on by the Danites to make a prognostication concerning their endeavors, he makes a political rather than spiritual response.

And when again confronted by the Danites, he is told to "put your hand over your mouth," which he does, ending any possibility of the Word of God being spoken.

I know of ministers today who fit this mold. And so do you. We could both name names. But it seems better not to. After all, could our names be on that list? In either case, let us pray.

Unholy Conquest (Judges 18:7–10, 27–28)

The names move slowly by: Laish. Bethlehem. Wounded Knee. Rosewood. *Shoah.* My Lai. Jonestown. Uganda. Afghanistan. How long will the innocent suffer? As long as the powerful pour the name of God like ketchup over their unholy conquests. And get away with it because we remain silent.

The Danites were, like the boll weevil of folk music, looking for a home. We already know from 1:34 that Dan had been driven into the mountains by the Amorites, away from water and fertile soil. Later, in the Samson story, we find out that the Danites suffered from their proximity to the Philistines. That they had no place to live (18:1) we might surmise from the most famous Danite, Samson, who was homeless. So we are ready to feel sympathetic toward the Danites. We wish for them to find a home. So how do they find one? They search out a quiet, peaceful, unsuspecting people, with no defense and no one to come to their aid, and they kill them all, burn their town of Laish, and take their land. Our sympathy boils away. So does that of the narrator. The text does not let this travesty pass in silence. It reminds us, in closing the story, that the Danites set up the stolen idol in their own shrine "until the land went into captivity" (18:30). This is to say that neither their unholy conquest nor their unholy shrine lasted for long.[19] God is not mocked.

The Nazis said that Germany was only looking for a little lebensraum in World War II. Serbia was simply trying to gather land necessary for a "Greater Serbia" in the recent Balkan war. Americans use nicer language, such as "manifest destiny" to describe the stealing of land and the killing of people. Recently, the Taliban in Afghanistan destroyed millennia-old statues of Buddha in an insane explosion of religious fundamentalism.

As if this is not enough, they were doing so in the name of God. Don't we always?

Can we still say that God is not mocked?

CHAPTER 10

The Levite's Wife—Not Every Story Has a Happy Ending

Judges 19–21

We have come to the end—literally. The book of Judges, which began so optimistically, comes to an end with these three chapters, having disintegrated into rape, murder, and civil war. There is no king in Israel and no law. People do whatever they want, however cruel or ungodly. We search desperately for a word of hope, something that will redeem the terror and sin through which we have traveled. And I mean this seriously. I am a preacher, and I am deeply vested in happy endings. I cheer lines like "It's Friday. But Sunday's coming!"[1] I readily adopted Eugene Boring's line about the meaning of the book of Revelation, in which he said "The point of Revelation is that everything is going to be all right,"[2] and applied that optimism to the whole Bible and to my view of the world. I once was so upset with a chapter of James Michener's *Poland,* in which a young man is brutally murdered and the woman he loves carried off into slavery, that I sat down and spent the better part of three days rewriting the chapter. I still have it, and frankly, I think my version is better than Michener's. But no one will ever know, except for you. I do not think I am just being unrealistic. I know that "all true stories end in death."[3] I just believe in heaven.

And yet it is a long way from Judges to heaven. Judges is broken, and I cannot fix it. I can rewrite Judges as I did Michener, but I would then be guilty of the very thing I seek to avoid. In my attempt to write violence out of the text, I would be doing violence to the text. So I finally have to admit that not all stories have happy endings. I heard of a man who went to see the film *Titanic* over and over again, each time hoping that the ship would not sink. Searching for a happy ending to this period in the life of Israel is doomed to the same failure.

The question then becomes: can a community of faith learn not only from good news but also from bad news? I believe the answer is yes. And the issues at stake are not just literary but theological. At the beginning of the book of Judges the people look to God for advice (1:1). At the end of the book (21:19) the people continue to praise God in the midst of their trouble. The one constant, in and out of season, is God. Even if they misunderstand God's will, the people continue to accept that the central fact of their lives is God. In spite of everything, that is good news.

Honor Gone Wrong (Judges 19–21)

Few words set hearts aflutter more than *honor,* especially when delivered in patriotic speeches accompanied by bagpipes. Shakespeare had King Richard II say, "Take honour from me, and my life is done."[4] More recently we may recall the lines of Stephen Spender quoted by Edward Kennedy at the funeral of his brother Robert:

> Born of the sun, they travelled a short while towards
>   the sun,
> And left the vivid air signed with their honour.[5]

Honor is a good thing. But sometimes honor goes wrong. People may not understand it, but they will quite willingly die for it. They will also kill others for it. As this is being written in the twenty-first century, honor has once again spun out of control. A recent article noted, for example, that "in more and more countries, women are being killed because they are perceived to have shamed their families."[6] These so-called "honor killings" have recently been observed in India, Pakistan, Bangladesh, Turkey, Peru, Jordan, and Israel, among others. They have also been recorded in such Western countries as

Britain, Norway, and Italy. Why is this happening? As one professor of religion put it:

> To these men who are killing their wives and sisters, their honor is something that is priceless, and the lives of these women are worth very little. Women are replaceable [in their view], but honor is not.[7]

Witness this excerpt from a recent interview with two Pakistani men, father and son, on *Nightline*:

Father: My daughter ran away with someone, so we killed them both.

Olenka Frankiel: You killed your own daughter?

Father: Yes.

Olenka Frankiel: Why?

Father: When she eloped, she wasn't my daughter anymore. I did the right thing. I'm an honorable man. I killed them both.

Olenka Frankiel: Is it honorable to kill your daughter?

Father: There is no greater honor anywhere.

Olenka Frankiel (voice-over)**:** It was the girl's brother who'd fired the fatal shot on the orders of his father.

Son: I am proud and ashamed.

Olenka Frankiel: How can you be proud and ashamed at the same time? Which is it?

Son: I'm proud that I killed her, but ashamed that she was my sister.[8]

Killers like these often go unpunished. How can this be? What is the basis for such a perverted sense of honor? It is something that runs deeply and persistently within the human psyche. "I am somebody. I am to be respected." So far so good. But it doesn't stop there. It goes on. "Anyone who shows disrespect to me (my tribe, my nation), who challenges my (our) standing in the community (world), will answer to me. I will preserve or regain my (our) honor by making them recant.

If they will not, it is my right to fight against them and kill them if necessary." Somewhere along that trajectory, a good thing goes wrong.

Picture this. You are living in Bethlehem about three thousand years ago. One day you see a crowd coming down the street toward your house, following a man who is carrying a parcel in his arms. When they have gathered before your door, the man, a messenger, begins to tell a story, but before he finishes, you know what has happened. And the memories come.

She was a lovely child, full of energy and life, and she grew gracefully into womanhood. When the Levite came to town as a suitor, you welcomed him. Even though he sought her as his *pilegesh* or secondary wife, you thought it would still be a good situation for her and especially for you. He was a man of stature and substance, able to pay a handsome bride price, and you quickly agreed to the match.

Some months later you were astonished to find your daughter back at your doorstep, with tears running down from blackened eyes onto dusty cheeks. She said that the Levite had beaten her until she could not take it any more, and so she finally had returned to the only sanctuary she knew, the home of her girlhood, the home of her father.[9] You were distressed, of course, that she had been beaten, but you also knew that the conventional wisdom of your time suggested that when women were beaten by husbands, it was because they deserved it. And most of all, you were distressed that the Levite could now reclaim his bride price, money that you had already committed to projects that would greatly increase your wealth and respect in Bethlehem. So you told your daughter she could come into the house, but only through the servants' quarters, because she belonged with her husband and had no right to be here without him. As she retreated from the threshold and walked around to the back, your primary thoughts were: (1) what had your daughter done to cause you such loss of face, and (2) would the Levite want his money back?

You were still worrying over these questions when the Levite showed up four months later. But he had a smile on his face, saying that it had all been just a misunderstanding. You treated him grandly, wining and dining him for some days and sending your daughter back with him with strict instructions to be loving and submissive, to do anything he asked of her. As they left, the Levite riding the donkey with your daughter walking behind, she turned back and looked at you. It was the last time you would ever see her face, and that look of resignation did not rest easily with you.

The messenger continues to tell how the Levite and your daughter had stopped for the night in Gibeah, hosted by a stranger. A group of Benjaminite ruffians sought to kill the Levite. But the host pleaded with the gang and pushed your daughter out the door instead. All night long they raped and abused her, finally tossing her like a bag of dirty laundry before the door of the house where they were staying. She managed to crawl far enough to gain the doorstep of the house, but fell unconscious and died reaching for the threshold. (The Levite had not told the messenger that your daughter was offered to the mob to protect him not from murder but homosexual rape, which would have dishonored him. Nor did he say that after your daughter was thrown to the wolves, he went to bed, and when he awoke in the morning and found your daughter by the doorstep, his only words to her were "Get up! Let's go."[10])

The messenger finishes by saying that when the Levite got home, he cut your daughter into twelve pieces and sent the pieces throughout Israel, asking for help to restore his honor. He unwraps the parcel, which holds the right arm of your daughter, and lays it across the threshold.[11] She has finally come home. The gathered crowd murmurs its willingness to help the Levite get his honor restored. You wonder if he is also going to want his money back.

Soon after, all Israel gathers and wages war against the Benjaminites for the dishonor done to the Levite. The text lists 90,760 as killed and hints that the carnage is much greater. After the defeat of the Benjaminites, rather than have the decimated tribe disappear from among the tribes of Israel, the other tribes approve the destruction of Jabesh-gilead and the abduction of four hundred virgins to replenish the tribe. We suppose the Levite is satisfied with what has been done to restore his honor. The price of that honor, however, is high. And we doubt that the Levite's wife and the other hundred thousand or so that have been slaughtered and the hundreds who were abducted see the exchange as equitable: one man's honor for the death and rape of so many.

The story of the Levite's wife, which precipitated the civil war that closes the book of Judges, is even more horrible than it seems. We recoil against the abuse, vainglory, rape, murder, lies, and dismemberment. But lest we forget, this whole story is about honor. We have, since our childhood, been told that honor is a great thing and that the price of honor is high, but is it this high? A hundred thousand to one? And lest we forget again, this story marks the conclusion of the downward spiral of the book of Judges. This is rock bottom. This is idolatry of the worst kind. Only this time the idol is not foreign or silver; the idol is one man's and one people's misguided sense of honor. The people treat each other shamefully, not honorably. Even the picture of God is skewed into that of a bumbling war god.

Thank goodness this story is three thousand years old and not contemporary. Thank goodness we do not do this kind of thing any more, do we? Well, ask the women who have been killed because they resisted their father's choice of a husband for them, because they looked at a man in "the wrong way," because they didn't cook the chicken right, bringing dishonor upon their families.

It is certainly true that the rest of the world can act in a pretty uncivilized manner. But thank goodness we don't do this kind of thing in North America, do we? Well, the brilliant writer Robertson Davies relates this story about his grandmother Malvina in *Murther and Walking Spirits*:

> At seventeen she had suffered from "a gathered throat" which the doctor diagnosed as tonsils, and said that they must come out. So one Saturday (after work), she made her way to the doctor's office, and he removed her tonsils, without anaesthetic, for, as he explained, it was a quick operation and the discomfort trivial.

> Walking home afterward, spitting blood into her handkerchief, she was overcome with pain and weakness and collapsed against a green picket fence,

vomiting blood and losing consciousness. The woman who was sitting on the *stoep* behind the fence hastened to her assistance, took her into the house, and sent a message to [her father]. In due course he arrived with the family horse-and-buggy, and took his daughter home, refusing to speak to the kindly woman. And when he reached home his wrath, and his wife's, was terrible.

If Malvina had to faint, did she have to do it outside Kate Lake's? A known house of ill-fame, where Kate Lake kept shameless girls who did unspeakable things for men of low character…She had allowed herself to be taken up onto the *stoep* of that house where the Lord knows who might see her! Moral indignation clouded [their] home for days to follow.[12]

She had crossed the wrong threshold.

At least this story is almost a hundred years old. Fortunately, as we enter the twenty-first century, we have outgrown such behavior, have we not? Well, how often do we read it in our newspapers? Every week at least. Sometimes every day. After years of abuse, a woman divorces her husband. Saying that if he cannot have her, no one can have her, he then kills her and finishes the story by killing himself, feeling that in these two acts, his "honor" is restored. There are, of course, gentler ways of reclaiming lost manhood and lost honor. One of the leaders of the Promise Keepers movement puts it this way:

The first thing you do is sit down with your wife and say something like this: "Honey, I've made a terrible mistake. I've given you my role. I gave up leading this family, and I forced you to take my place. Now I must reclaim that role."

Don't misunderstand what I'm saying here. I'm not suggesting that you *ask* for your role back, I'm urging you to *take it back*.[13]

A gentler approach, yes. But a gentleness that does not renounce violence may be no gentleness at all.

There are three things the church can say in the face of such distortions of honor, here and around the world, and two of them we can learn from the book of Judges. First, these acts are idolatrous. They are against God. And second, these perversions of honor are not the maintenance of tradition, but rather, the symbol of a disintegrating society, a culture falling apart. Honor of this sort is a vestige of a patriarchal world. We think it is disappearing, but it remains very persistent and very deadly. Rape as a physical and psychological weapon in the recent Balkan conflict was particularly brutal. Jerome Socolovsky writes:

> As long as [people] have waged war, rape has been an outrageous weapon in [their] arsenal. And as long as [people] have sought to punish war crimes, rape has been near the bottom of [their] list. An international tribunal, which has been investigating Balkan war crimes, wants to turn things around. A rape trial opening [in The Hague] marks the first time an international court tackles sexual enslavement.[14]

A faint glimmer of hope in the dark side of human discord.[15]

Finally, the church can learn something from the example of Jesus. Jesus did not seek honor. Living honorably is one thing. Holding your honor as the highest good and being willing to fight, kill, and die rather than lose face is not what Jesus did. And it is not what Jesus would do. Jesus did not die for his honor or ours. He died for the sins of the world. David Buttrick writes:

> Jesus seemed to refuse all forms of social approval. He made no attempt to dazzle crowds: after miracles, he cautioned silence. He did not try to please a social elite, to be in with the in-group. He did not try to get anywhere, have anything, or be anybody—all normal grounds for social endorsement. He did not even try to fulfill anyone's messianic dreams. Instead, throughout his life there was an unswerving dedication to God's will: "Not my will, but yours be done," he prayed. As a result, he was not a respected member of society.[16]

We all have conflicts, people and nations. We might lose face. We might have to give the money back. But something greater than these is at stake. When we feel we have been disrespected—"dissed" in today's vernacular, cut off in traffic, not valued at work, what shall we do? Strike back? Make them pay? Or perhaps we can stop and realize that doing God's will is more important than strutting our own stuff. Hastening the coming reign of God brings more joy than being "somebody" in this world.

We have looked three thousand years in the past. Now let us look into the future. How long? We don't know. But not long.

> After this I looked, and there was a great multitude that no one could count, from every nation, from all tribes and peoples and languages, standing before the throne, and before the Lamb, robed in white, with palm branches in their hands. They cried out in a loud voice, saying,
>
> "Salvation belongs to our God who is seated on the throne, and to the Lamb."
>
> And all the angels stood around the throne and around the elders and the four living creatures, and they fell on their faces before the throne and worshiped God, singing,
>
> "Amen! Blessing and glory and wisdom
> and thanksgiving and honor
> and power and might
> be to our God forever and ever! Amen."
> (Revelation 7:9–12)

We will be there before the throne, it says, all of us. Which means we will have finally crossed the threshold, the Levite's wife and all of us. We will finally have come home. And there we will find that our posture is not one of being seated in the high place of honor, but flat on our faces, worshiping God. The text makes it clear:

"Honor belongs to God."
Amen.

To Protect and to Serve (Judges 21:20–25)

In 1984, an African American artist named Kimako Baraka was brutally and senselessly murdered. Her brother Amiri preached her funeral, and in it he said:

Kimako made the ultimate mistake of wanting to be a creative force in this rotten society. Of being moved by truth and beauty. Of wanting to do nothing so much as dance, to express the rhythm of life as a part of that rhythm...Kimako's crime for which [she was] destroyed, was wanting to be genuinely human, in spite of the madness that passes as sanity and respectability... Our failure is that we have not created a context in which life can live, in which creativity can be spared and developed, that we have not built a world in which something wonderful and blessed, Kimako Baraka, could exist, where life would be sacred and protected...My gentle, fragile sister is dead because we failed to protect her.[17]

"Because we failed to protect her." Baraka's condemnation of our society is, like the old spiritual, deep and wide. It reaches to the depths of our social systems and to the far boundaries of our life together. For one way in which societies are measured is how they protect those least able to protect themselves: the very young and the very old, the disabled and the gentle, those who live in fear, afraid to open the door. One large American police department has its slogan written on every squad car: "To protect and to serve." That we need such a force serves to remind us of the danger of anarchy.

Another reminder comes from the end of Judges, for Israel has itself fallen into anarchy, as we have seen. There are no more judges. There is no king. "All the people did what was right in their own eyes" (21:25). The lack of protection for those who need it is modeled in this book primarily by women. The first woman mentioned in the book is Achsah, a strong and assertive person. From there the situation goes downhill, finally spinning out of control into human sacrifice, rape, murder, and dismemberment. In the Samson story we see the bitter irony of a woman being burned who sought to protect herself from burning.[18] No one else, including her husband Samson, sought to protect her. As the book ends, one tribe, decimated in battle, abducts hundreds of young women as wives, kidnapping and rape having become acceptable ways of obtaining wives. Tammi Schneider writes that these women's tragic plight shows how Israelite society had disintegrated to the point that institutional rape was condoned and "the system of protection was intentionally destroyed."[19] The fathers and brothers of the women stood by and did nothing after they were assured by the abductors that the kidnapping would not dishonor them.

A more recent example of this failure is found in the history of Christianity in Samoa. In pre-Christian Samoa women held an important position in Samoan society, which came from the concept of *feagaiga*. *Feagaiga* literally meant "covenant" and referred to the covenant of respect that existed between a brother and a sister. The brother was obligated to serve and protect his sister, married or not, for as long as he lived. But after the missionaries came, this respect was transferred to the missionaries, and the status of women declined precipitously.[20] This unintended consequence of the church's missionary activity in Samoa reminds us of the danger proclaimed by the narrator of Judges: when the social structures of a society crumble, the protections those structures offer also fall away, and the poorest and weakest are always the ones who suffer.

As I write this, the second-fastest-selling album of all time has just been given a music award for its lyrics.[21] What are the lyrics about? Rape and murder. We must be careful about looking down our noses at the actions of the archaic folk in the old book of Judges. How much better are we doing? Have we not been warned that those who ignore history are doomed to repeat it? Have we not heard the stories from Judges? If "what is right in our own eyes" is not measured against some theological and ethical standard, we too will descend into selfishness and anarchy. We will fail to protect those among us least able to protect themselves. And years or centuries from now people will read our stories and shake their heads, saying "How mean, how stupid, how faithless they were at the beginning of the third millennium!"

I would rather they say, "They read the stories from Judges. They learned. They changed."

Which shall it be?

Conclusion

The journey through Judges is not an easy one, but neither is it without benefit. To reprise the two central questions of this book: why and how should we preach from Judges? Perhaps the strongest rationales for Judges-based sermons are the timeliness of the stories and the gateways they provide for an examination of our relationships with God and one another. As I have said, Judges is crisis literature, and there are more crises boiling today than just international terrorism. Early in his commentary on Judges in the Interpretation series, Hebrew Bible scholar J. Clinton McCann proffers the following list of concerns:

- Tension and strife between rival groups (in the Middle East or elsewhere)
- Disputes over land and territory
- Uncertainty over the roles of men and women
- Power-hungry political leaders
- Child abuse
- Spouse abuse
- Senseless and excessive violence
- Male political leaders who chase women
- Excessive individualism
- Moral confusion
- Social chaos

McCann then asks, perceptively, "What time and place is being described by this list?"[1] Then? Now? Both? Or, sadly, all times and places?

I have been flooded in the past few weeks with sermons preached by former students and friends on Sundays following September 11, 2001. They are, collectively, some of the best sermons I have read in years. Crisis sermons are difficult to prepare and preach, but they also seem to call forth the best we have. None of them was Judges-based, which did not surprise me, because so few people think of Judges as a source or ground for sermons. Perhaps this book can change that.

How does one use the vignettes and sermons I have gathered here? Some of the ideas and stories may be useful as primary or supportive material in a variety of sermons, not only those grounded in Judges. But even if not, the analogical model I used may call forth stories and experiences from the reader's own treasure that are far beyond my knowing. It has been said that analogy may not be a good way of gaining understanding, but it is the best way we have. Asking what can function in our world as do these stories from Judges in post-exodus, pre-monarchical Israel, can lead to stirred imaginations, vivid images, and new ideas about living in covenant with God and one another.[2]

I also encourage preachers to move beyond prosaic interpretation to allow texts the freedom to speak God's word to us in a variety of ways. And finally, let us remember that as difficult as the relationship was between God and God's people during that time and as horrible as some of the experiences were that they shared together, the relationship survived.

So can ours.

Introduction

[1]D. T. Niles, cited in David Black, "The Calling," *New York Times Magazine,* 11 May 1986, 38.

[2]Meir Sternberg, cited in Marc Brettler, "Never the Twain Shall Meet? The Ehud Story as History and Literature," *Hebrew Union College Annual* 42 (Cincinnati, 1991): 285.

[3]Ronald E. Osborn, *The Spirit of American Christianity* (New York: Harper & Bros., 1958): 143–44.

[4]Osborn went on to say that his analogy was not meant to demean academic theology or major movements, only to indicate that the popular faith, unsystematic though it may be, is there as a wholesome and vital force.

[5]David Jobling, "Structuralist Criticism: The Text's World of Meaning," in *Judges and Method: New Methods in Biblical Studies,* ed. Gale A. Yee (Minneapolis: Fortress Press, 1995), 112.

[6]Of course, Jobling was speaking as a scholar to other scholars in his chapter.

[7]Most Bibles call this woman the Levite's "concubine." She is a *pilegesh,* a legitimate wife of secondary rank. As J. Cheryl Exum has pointed out to me in personal correspondence, to call her a "concubine" in English is to prejudice the reader against her unfairly. I shall not add to that prejudice. For more information, see Andrew H. Mayes, "Deuteronomistic Royal Ideology in Judges 17–21," *Biblical Interpretation* 9:3 (2001), 241 n. 1.

[8]Ian Macpherson, *Kindling* (Old Tappan, N.J.: Fleming H. Revell, 1969); Halford Luccock, *Unfinished Business: Short Diversions on More than 100 Religious Themes* (New York: Harper & Bros., 1956).

[9]Paul Scott Wilson, *The Practice of Preaching* (Nashville: Abingdon Press, 1995), 145. In conversation with the author, Wilson expanded this affirmation to suggest that when an individual text leaves such an impression, we need to measure it against the clear and compelling message of the entire Bible. I agree.

[10]See also Joseph R. Jeter, Jr., "Ruth People in an Esther World," *Patterns of Preaching: A Sermon Sampler,* ed. Ronald J. Allen (St. Louis: Chalice Press, 1998), 51–56. For a good introduction to intertextuality, see *Reading Between Texts: Intertextuality and the Hebrew Bible,* ed. Danna Nolan Fewell (Louisville: Westminster John Knox Press, 1992).

[11]Danna Nolan Fewell, "Deconstructive Criticism: Achsah and the (E)razed City of Writing," in *Judges and Method,* 131–32.

[12]See J. Cheryl Exum, ed., *Virtual History and the Bible* (Leiden: Brill, 2000).

[13]Among useful studies are Dipesh Chakrebarty, "A Small History of Subaltern Studies," in *A Companion to Postcolonial Studies,* ed. Henry Schwarz and S. Ray (Oxford: Blackwell, 2000), 467–85; Stephen D. Moore,

"Postcolonialism," in *Handbook of Postmodern Biblical Interpretation,* ed. A. K. M. Adam (St. Louis: Chalice Press, 2000), 182–88; Musa Dube, *Postcolonial Feminist Interpretation of the Bible* (St. Louis: Chalice Press, 2000); and Fernando F. Segovia, ed., *Interpreting Beyond Borders* (Sheffield: Sheffield Academic Press, 2000).

[14]Perhaps the best known of these works is *The Bible Unearthed* by Israel Finkelstein and Neil Asher Silberman (New York: Free Press, 2001), although earlier investigation was done by scholars such as George Mendenhall and Norman Gottwald.

[15]E. K. Brown, cited in Patrick J. Willson and Beverly Roberts Gaventa, "Preaching as the Re-reading of Scripture," *Interpretation* 52:4 (October 1998): 393.

[16]Thomas H. Troeger, *Ten Strategies for Preaching in a Multi-media Culture* (Nashville: Abingdon Press, 1996), 16–17.

[17]Fewell, "Deconstructive Criticism," 141.

[18]See Ronald E. Osborn, "A Functional Definition of Preaching," *Encounter* 37:1 (Winter 1976): 53–54, 65–67.

Chapter 1: Why Preach from Judges?

[1]Martin Noth, *Überlieferungsgeschichtliche Studien* (Halle, 1943), partially translated into English by a team of scholars and published under the title *The Deuteronomistic History* (Sheffield: JSOT Press, 1981).

[2]The period of the judges, according to internal evidence, is 480 years. But external evidence points to a timeframe as short as 150 years (1200–1050 B.C.E.). See Dennis T. Olson, "The Book of Judges" in *The New Interpreter's Bible,* vol. 2 (Nashville: Abingdon Press, 1998), 724, and Paul Enns, *Bible Study Commentary: Judges* (Grand Rapids: Zondervan, 1982), 8.

[3]Jon Berquist suggests that *shophet* can also be understood as "bringer of justice," *Reclaiming Her Story: The Witness of the Women in the Old Testament* (St. Louis: Chalice Press, 1992), 91.

[4]Phyllis Trible, *Texts of Terror* (Philadelphia: Fortress Press, 1984).

[5]Ibid., xiii.

[6]Elisabeth Schüssler Fiorenza, cited in Claudia V. Camp, "Feminist Theological Hermeneutics: Canon and Christian Identity," in *Searching the Scriptures–Volume One: A Feminist Introduction,* ed. Elisabeth Schüssler Fiorenza (New York: Crossroad, 1993), 159.

[7]Barnabas Lindars, *Interpreting Judges Today* (London: Univ. of London Press, 1983), 1.

[8]George Dennison, "In Praise of What Persists," in *In Praise of What Persists,* ed. Stephen Berg, (New York: Harper, 1983), 69–92.

[9]I will never forget a letter I received in seminary from Bible professor Walter Wink (written April 27, 1970) in response to my sophomoric attack on the relevance of scripture. Among other things, he said, "I don't agree that other works say 'more' to our lives than the Bible. I accept as a valid working hypothesis the idea of the canon, whereby all my experience is filtered through the gospel message as I seek to understand my own existence under Christ. So that while *One Flew Over the Cuckoo's Nest* is in my view a better exposition of the meaning of the Passion than *Hebrews,* I *see* this only because I am constantly interacting with the biblical message (which includes *Hebrews).*" Wink was right. It just took me a while to see that.

[10]Alexander Procter, in Joseph R. Jeter, Jr., *Alexander Procter: The Sage of Independence* (Claremont, Calif.: Disciples Seminary Foundation, 1983), 102.

[11]I first heard this from Ronald Osborn. I have seen several variations of Robinson's assurance. Edwin Gaustad has Robinson say "the Lord hath more truth and light yet to break forth out of his holy Word" in *A Religious History of America* (New York: Harper & Row, 1966), 47.

[12]Arthur John Gossip, "But When Life Tumbles In, What Then?" in *The Hero in Thy Soul* (Edinburgh: T. & T. Clark, 1928), 110.

[13]I find three comments from women on this text to be particularly enlightening. Imagine Sarah waking up one morning to find Abraham and Isaac gone. Days pass. Her worry increases. Finally, late one afternoon she sees them dragging back toward home. Then imagine her saying, "Where have you been?" Pause. "You did what?" Ellen M. Umansky creates such a scene in "Re-Visioning Sarah: A Midrash on Genesis 22," in *Four Centuries of Jewish Women's Spirituality*, ed. Ellen M. Umansky and Dianne Ashton (Boston: Beacon Press, 1992), 235. I have also heard of a feminist who nevertheless uses masculine language for God, saying that she does so based on this text. God is certainly male, she says. No woman would ever require such a thing. I regret that I failed to document the source. Then, about God saying to Abraham, "Take your son, your only son," J. Cheryl Exum remarks, "Of course Isaac is *not* his only son." Did God forget about Ishmael? Jon Berquist also offers an interesting approach to this text in suggesting that the text is a test to see not whether Abraham will kill Isaac but rather whether or not Abraham will argue with God. Moses argued. Sarah argued. Why was Abraham willing to give up his son without an argument? See *Reclaiming Her Story*, 45–47. Berquist also offers the pointed reminder that we cannot afford the equation "Hebrew Bible God=wrathful, but New Testament God= gracious," especially if God is in charge of everything, since God thinks about killing a main character's son in the Old Testament, and almost does it, but in the New Testament, God actually goes through with it (from personal correspondence with Berquist, August 22, 2001). Finally, a friend made the following interpretative suggestion, seriously I think, about the text. "Since the whole future of the Judeo-Christian faith is at stake in this story," he said, "perhaps the lesson is the wisdom of God in choosing Abraham and not Joey Jeter to live out the lesson." Point taken.

[14]Ronald J. Allen, *Interpreting the Gospel* (St. Louis: Chalice, 1998), 82–95. See also Allen's earlier article "Preaching against the Text," *Encounter* 48 (Winter 1987): 105–15.

[15]Phyllis Trible, *Genesis 22: The Sacrifice of Sarah* (Valparaiso, Ind.: Valparaiso Univ. Press, 1990), 15.

[16]I note that playwright Eve Ensler denies that violence against women is an "issue." It is, rather, she says, the "central thread [of] everything." Cited in Elysa Gardner, "Ensler Takes Aim at Patriarchy," *USA Today*, 29 Nov 2001, 18D.

[17]This affirmation of Barth's has become part of contemporary theological *lingua franca*. But it is not representative of the "whole" Barth. Although he was very much involved in politics and social issues, there was something about the faith that he kept separate. Barth once wrote of sermons, "Application…does not always have to be *à jour*. We do not always have to bring in the latest and most sensational events. For instance, if a fire broke out in the community last week, and church members are still suffering under

its awful impact, we should be on guard against even hinting at this theme in the sermon. It belongs to everyday life, but now it is Sunday." From *Homiletics: The Nature and Preparation of the Sermon,* trans. Geoffrey W. Bromily with Donald E. Daniels (unpublished ms.), cited in David Buttrick, "Preaching, Hermeneutics and Liberation," in *Standing with the Poor,* ed. Paul P. Park (Cleveland: Pilgrim Press, 1992), 106. I have spent a great deal of time studying crisis preaching, and I find this remark of Barth's astonishing. But I keep it at footnote level, lest I be accused of faulting my better.

[18]See Joseph R. Jeter, Jr., *Crisis Preaching* (Nashville: Abingdon Press, 1998), 10, 101.

[19]See Henri J. M. Nouwen, *The Wounded Healer* (Garden City: Doubleday, 1972).

[20]Ibid., 95.

[21]Thomas H. Troeger, *Ten Strategies for Preaching in a Multi-media Culture* (Nashville: Abingdon Press, 1996), 97.

[22]Harry Emerson Fosdick, "What's the Matter with Preaching?" *Harper's Magazine* 157 (July 1928): 135.

[23]Hebrew Bible scholar J. Clinton McCann graciously shared with me his manuscript on Judges for the Interpretation series before it was published. I am very much in his debt. In McCann's section on "Theology in the Book of Judges," he seems determined to exonerate God from all the horrible things that happen in Judges. He writes, "God's sovereignty takes the form of steadfast love. Israel's God is essentially gracious and merciful" (J. Clinton McCann, *Judges,* Interpretation: A Bible Commentary for Preaching and Teaching [Louisville: Westminster John Knox Press, 2003], 36). Although I believe both these affirmations, I do not believe that the stories in Judges substantiate them. For another perspective, see David Penchansky, *What Rough Beast? Images of God in the Hebrew Bible* (Louisville: Westminster John Knox Press, 1999).

[24]Aaron Sorkin, "Two Cathedrals," *The West Wing,* May 16, 2001. Used with permission.

[25]The Grimm brothers' fairy tale world was not always wonderful. Some of their tales are as horrific as some of the stories in Judges.

Chapter 2: The Failed Conquest of Canaan

[1]*The Cedar Hill (Texas) Sentinel,* 20 January 2000, 6.

[2]Leviticus 24:20.

[3]Dennis T. Olson, "The Book of Judges," in *The New Interpreter's Bible,* vol. 2 (Nashville: Abingdon Press, 1998), 737.

[4]More about the "town of books" can be found on the official Web site: www.hay-on-wye.co.uk.

[5]President Donald Shriver of Union Theological Seminary in New York during a 1970s address.

[6]See Dubravko Kakarigi, "Views of the National Library," 1994, found online at http://www.kakarigi.net/manu/vijecnic.htm. My colleague Laurie Feille first told me of this horrifying deed.

[7]Sally Webster, cited by Katherine Roth, "Valuable Art Lost in WTC Rubble," *Los Angeles Times,* 22 September 2001, 2.

[8]Danna Nolan Fewell, "Deconstructive Criticism: Achsah and the (E)razed City of Writing," in *Judges and Method: New Methods in Biblical Studies,* ed. Gale A. Yee (Minneapolis: Fortress Press, 1995), 131–32.

⁹Lillian Klein, "Achsah: What Price This Prize," in *Judges: A Feminist Companion to the Bible (Second Series)*, ed. Athalya Brenner (Sheffield: Sheffield Academic Press, 1999), 19–20.

¹⁰See James E. Altenbaumer, "The View from the Mountaintop," in *Preaching through the Apocalypse*, ed. Cornish Rogers and Joseph Jeter (St. Louis: Chalice Press, 1992), 147–48.

¹¹Judges 1:12–15 and an almost verbatim duplicate of the story in Joshua 15:16–19.

¹²For example, Klein, "Achsah," 18–26; Fewell, "Deconstructive Criticism," 129–42; Susan Ackerman, *Warrior, Dancer, Seductress, Queen* (New York: Doubleday, 1998), 1–3, 6, 290–91.

¹³A stronger reading than the NRSV's "Give me a present." See Klein, "Achsah," 25.

¹⁴Klein, "Achsah," 26.

¹⁵There are interesting parallels to Achsah's quest for water in the story of Hagar's thirst in Genesis 21 and the gift of water in Isaiah 55.

¹⁶John Nichols, *The Milagro Beanfield War* (New York: Holt, Rinehart and Winston, 1974), 21–22.

¹⁷Ibid.

¹⁸The response of television evangelists Jerry Falwell and Pat Robertson to the horrors of September 11, 2001, resembles the rationale of the writer of Judges. "God will not be mocked," Falwell said.

> God continues to lift the curtain and allow the enemies of America to give us probably what we deserve...The pagans, and the abortionists, and the feminists, and the gays and the lesbians who are actively trying to make that an alternative lifestyle, the ACLU, the People for the American Way–all of them who have tried to secularize America– I point the finger in their face and say, 'You helped this happen.'" (Jerry Falwell, in John Harris, "God Gave U.S. 'What We Deserve,' Falwell Says," *Washington Post*, 14 September 2001)

Picture Falwell and Robertson talking together some three thousand years ago. One of them might have said, "Why did God let such terrible things happen to us? Because we mingled with the Canaanites!" I also remember painfully how we arrived at the convention center in Kansas City on July 13, 2001, for the joint Synod/Assembly of the United Church of Christ and the Christian Church (Disciples of Christ), only to be greeted by a group of protesters under the leadership of Rev. Fred Phelps, pastor of the Westboro Baptist Church of Topeka, Kansas. They were holding up a variety of signs, the nicest of which said, "God hates fags." Such sad action finds part of its support in a xenophobic reading of scripture.

¹⁹See Ackerman, *Warrior, Dancer*, 135–36.

Chapter 3: The Rise of the Judges

¹I have puzzled over how to render the Tetragrammaton. "Yahweh" or "YHWH" would be troublesome for some readers, and "Hashem" is all but unknown in Christian circles. To say "God" is to undermine the particularity of the text, for there are many names in the Bible for God. I have finally decided to follow the NRSV and use LORD in all capitals. I realize this too is not without problems.

[2]Marvin Tate, cited in J. Clinton McCann, *Judges,* Interpretation: A Bible Commentary for Preaching and Teaching (Louisville: Westminster John Knox Press, 2003), 45–46, 136.

[3]A few days before this was written, a woman and her seven-month-old baby were killed by a Peruvian jet fighter that mistook the missionary plane in which they were flying for a drug-running plane. It saddened me to hear her husband at her funeral call this tragedy-cum-murder "the plan of God."

[4]This description is also found in 2:11, 3:12, 4:1, 6:1, 10:6, and 13:1.

[5]This cycle is taken from David Jobling, "Structuralist Criticism: The Text's World of Meaning," in *Judges and Method: New Methods in Biblical Studies,* ed. Gale A. Yee (Minneapolis: Fortress Press, 1995), 96. One might also mention how the texts frequently add that "The spirit of The LORD came upon" the judge in question. This is found in 3:10, 6:34, 11:29, 13:25 and 14:19.

[6]Peter Baelz, *St. Cuthbert: Yesterday and Today* (Durham, U.K.: Cannyprint Ltd., 1989), 4. A similar tale could be told about a Bohemian duke named Wenceslaus (d. 929), immortalized in John Mason Neale's Christmas song "Good King Wenceslaus."

[7]Dennis T. Olson, "The Book of Judges" in *The New Interpreter's Bible,* vol. 2 (Nashville: Abingdon Press, 1998), 767.

[8]Remember also that Othniel's wife Achsah has already shown her wise and clever ability to manage the family's business, agricultural, and perhaps religious affairs. Many leaders, both men and women, fail in their efforts through lack of a viable support system. Othniel appears to have been fortunate in his.

[9]Verse 24 tends to indicate that the cool chamber is a toilet. But Eglon would not have invited Ehud to a conference on the toilet. It is more likely that the toilet was in a smaller adjoining room.

[10]See, e.g., Lowell K. Handy, "Uneasy Laughter: Ehud and Eglon as Ethnic Humor," *Scandinavian Journal of the Old Testament* 6:2 (1992): 245.

[11]Baruch Halpern, "The Assassination of Eglon–the First Locked-Room Murder Mystery," *Bible Review* 4:6 (December 1988): 44.

[12]Ernst Axel Knauf, "Eglon and Ophrah: Two Toponymic Notes on the Book of Judges," *Journal for the Study of the Old Testament* 51 (September 1991): 29.

[13]*Die Bybel in praktyk* (Ventner: 1993), 331–32, cited by Ferdinand Deist, "'Murder in the Toilet' (Judges 3:12–30): Translation and Transformation," *Scriptura* 58 (1996): 267. See also Olson, "Book of Judges," 772.

[14]"Sovereign," words and arrangement by Carol Antrom (Philadelphia: Marbert, 1986).

[15]H. W. Hertzberg, *Die Bücher Josua, Richter, Ruth* (Goettingen: Vandenhoeck & Ruprecht, 1953), 166, cited by Deist, "Murder in the Toilet," 268.

[16]Renate Wind, *Dietrich Bonhoeffer: A Spoke in the Wheel,* trans. John Bowden (Grand Rapids, Mich.: Eerdmans, 1992), 144.

[17]See Handy, "Uneasy Laughter," 245.

[18]Ibid.

[19]Years ago I read a sermon of which only the title remains to me: "Dead Egyptians on the Shore." Using the death of so many not of our faith to make a positive theological point about our faith bothered me then and still does.

[20]Halpern, "Assassination of Eglon," 44.

[21]E. D. Grohman, "Moab," *Interpreter's Dictionary of the Bible* (Nashville: Abingdon Press, 1980), 3:418.

[22]Handy, "Uneasy Laughter," 244.

[23]Ibid., 245–46.

[24]Deist, "Murder in the Toilet," 271.

[25]Ibid.

[26]NBC pilot episode of *Sister Kate,* September 16, 1989, cited in Richard F. Wolff, "Prime Time Television's History of the American Church: A Critical Assessment," *Journal of Communication and Religion* 18, no. 2 (September 1995): 44–45.

[27]From an unpublished sermon manuscript entitled "I See Your Face" by Louis Wayne Stewart. Used with permission.

[28]David Gunn, lecture at Brite Divinity School, Fort Worth, Texas, 9 April 2000.

[29]Years ago I attempted to deal with this text homiletically, sharing two stories I can no longer document. In the first a guest minister preaches a sermon that disturbs a woman. The more she ponders, the angrier she gets. Finally she writes the man a scurrilous letter, which ends with the words: "Happy shall they be who take your little ones and dash them against the rock!"

The minister writes back, enclosing a picture of his children. "If you knew my little ones," he said, "and how precious they are, you would never in a million years have wished that fate upon them, however much you may disagree with me." She writes back, "You're right and I'm sorry. But can you understand how what *you* said made *me* feel?" He writes back, "Yes..."

And then she, and then he, and finally, reconciliation.

Then a Vietnamese refugee woman who had become a Christian was sitting in a Bible study group in her church when they came to this psalm. Nobody knew what to do with it, but they saw her eyes widen as she read. She told them that the boat she had been on trying to escape from Vietnam had been seized by pirates, and she watched as a man took her baby, dashed him against the side of the boat, and hurled him into the water. For a long time after, her most powerful feeling was the wish that someone would take that man's baby and dash it into the rocks. She suffered much guilt over that feeling until the morning in the Bible study when she heard someone else from beyond the ages express the same feelings in words that her new community called scripture. If people felt like that in the Bible, then maybe there was hope for her. And this song of anger became for her a song of freedom, as it had become for the first woman a song of reconciliation.

[30]John Muir, *John of the Mountains,* ed. Linnie Marsh Wolfe (Madison: Univ. of Wisconsin Press, 1979), 199.

[31]See David Buttrick, *Homiletic* (Philadelphia: Fortress Press, 1987), 138–39.

[32]Martin Noth, *The History of Israel* (New York: Harper & Row, 1960), 85–109. See Alan Hauser, "The 'Minor Judges'—A Re-evaluation," *Journal of Biblical Literature* 94:2 (June 1975): 190–200 for a critique of Noth. Mieke Bal in *Death and Dissymmetry* (Chicago: Univ. of Chicago Press, 1988) scoffs at Noth's theory.

[33]See E. Theodore Mullen, Jr., "The 'Minor Judges': Some Literary and Historical Considerations," *Catholic Biblical Quarterly* 44:2 (April 1982): 185–86.

[34]Noth would include only Tola, Jair, Ibzan, Elon, and Abdon in the list of minor judges, along with Jephthah, who is the one judge included in both groups.

[35]See McCann, *Judges,* 68–69.

[36]See Beverly Beem, "The Minor Judges: A Literary Reading of Some Very Short Stories," *The Biblical Canon in Comparative Perspective,* ed. K. Lawson Younger, Jr., et al. (Lewiston, N.Y.: Edwin Mellen Press, 1991), 164.

[37]"Rashi to Ezekiel 4:5," *The Tanakh,* Stone edition (Brooklyn: Mesorah, 1996), 588–89.

[38]See M. Eugene Boring, *Revelation* (Louisville: Westminster John Knox Press, 1989), 139.

[39]Dennis T. Olson, "The Book of Judges" in *The New Interpreter's Bible,* vol. 2 (Nashville: Abingdon Press, 1998), 840.

Chapter 4: Deborah, Barak, and Jael

[1]Dennis T. Olson, "The Book of Judges" in *The New Interpreter's Bible,* vol. 2 (Nashville: Abingdon Press, 1998), 787.

[2]John Knox, cited in Carol Blessing, "Judge, Prophet, Mother: Learning from Deborah," *Daughters of Sarah* 21:1 (Winter 1995): 35.

[3]See Danna Nolan Fewell and David M. Gunn, "Controlling Perspectives: Women, Men and Authority of Violence in Judges 4 & 5," in *Journal of the American Academy of Religion* 58:3 (Fall 1990): 397.

[4]See Priscilla Denham, "It's Hard to Sing the Song of Deborah," in *Spinning a Sacred Yarn: Women Speak from the Pulpit* (New York: Pilgrim Press, 1982), 63.

[5]Elizabeth Cady Stanton, *The Woman's Bible,* cited in Gale A. Yee, "By the Hand of a Woman: The Metaphor of the Woman-Warrior in Judges 4," *Semeia* 61 (1993): 123.

[6]Leonard Swidler, cited in Yee, "By the Hand," 123.

[7]"Navy Pilot who Opposed Women Fliers," *The Dallas Morning News* 20 August 1995, 9A.

[8]Ibid.

[9]Denham, "It's Hard to Sing," 62.

[10]If one includes the Apocrypha, there is a fifth, that of Judith.

[11]Mary's song has lines that are two syllables shorter and more regular than the others, which may show an assurance the others lack.

[12]Deborah's song is longer in this reading, as it is in scripture.

[13]See Psalm 96.

[14]Final paragraph revised from a previous sermon on this text published in the *Biblical Preaching Journal* (Fall 1996): 18–20.

[15]George Foot Moore, *A Critical and Exegetical Commentary on Judges* (New York: Charles Scribner's Sons, 1910), 146.

[16]Ibid.

[17]It is difficult for a speaker of modern English not to so translate, and in doing so not to remember Rudyard Kipling's rebuke:

You may talk o' gin an' beer
When you're quartered safe out 'ere
An' you're sent to penny-fights an' Aldershot it;
But when it comes to slaughter,
You will do your work on water.

An you'll lick the bloomin' boots of 'im that's got it.
—from "Gunga Din," in *Barrack-Room Ballads* (London: Methuen & Co., 1892), 23.

[18]William Shakespeare, *King Henry V,* act 4, scene 3, lines 66–75.

[19]One thinks also of other prophetic words, such as those from Amos, calling the wealthy to account.

[20]See comments by Stanton and Swidler cited earlier. See also Alice Ogden Bellis, "The Jael Enigma," in *Daughters of Sarah* 21:1 (Winter 1995), 19–20.

[21]See Yee, "By the Hand," 123. See also Fewell and Gunn, "Controlling Perspectives," 394–95.

[22]See Fewell and Gunn, "Controlling Perspectives," 392–94. See also Johanna W. H. Bos, "Out of the Shadows," in *Semeia* 42 (1988): 56–57, and Katherine Doob Sakenfeld, "Deborah, Jael and Sisera's Mother: Reading the Scriptures in Cross-cultural Context," in *Women, Gender and Christian Community,* ed. Jane Dempsey Douglass and James F. Kay (Louisville: Westminster John Knox Press, 1997), 19–21.

[23]Fewell and Gunn, "Controlling Perspectives," 395.

[24]Dan Via, *The Parables* (Philadelphia: Fortress Press, 1967), 159.

[25]Barnabas Lindars, "Deborah's Song: Women in the Old Testament," *Bulletin of John Rylands University Library of Manchester* 65:2 (Spring 1983): 164–65.

[26]Herman Herst, Jr, "Everyone Had a Mother," *Global Stamp News* (Nov. 1997): 6.

[27]Olson, "Book of Judges," 787.

[28]See Fokkelien van Dijk-Hemmes, "Mothers and a Mediator in the Song of Deborah," in *A Feminist Companion to Judges,* ed. Athalya Brenner (Sheffield: JSOT Press, 1993), 110–14.

[29]The line "a girl or two for every man" is even cruder in the Hebrew, "a womb [*rehem*] or two for every man." See Olson, "Book of Judges," 789.

[30]See Olson, "Book of Judges," 788; Susan Ackerman, *Warrior, Dancer, Seductress, Queen* (New York: Doubleday, 1998), 130; and J. Cheryl Exum, "Feminist Criticism: Whose Interests Are Being Served?" in *Judges and Method,* ed. Gale A. Yee (Minneapolis: Fortress Press, 1995), 73.

[31]Nehama Aschkenasy, *Woman at the Window* (Detroit: Wayne State Univ. Press, 1998).

[32]Ibid., 26.

[33]Paul Laurence Dunbar, "When Dey 'Listed Colored Soldiers," in *The Complete Poems of Paul Laurence Dunbar* (New York: Dodd, Mead & Co., 1967), 293–94.

[34]Ackerman writes significantly, "Judges 5 uses motherhood as a motif that holds its otherwise cataclysmic imagery in check. Motherhood, in this sense, becomes the theme that keeps the poem sane," *Warrior, Dancer,* 183.

[35]Sakenfeld, "Deborah, Jael, and Sisera's Mother," 22.

[36]Ibid.

Chapter 5: Gideon

[1]See D. W. Gooding, "The Composition of the Book of Judges," *Eretz-Israel* 16 (1982): 70–79; J. Paul Tanner, "The Gideon Narrative as the Focal Point of Judges," *Bibliotheca Sacra* 149 (Apr.-June 1992): 146–61, and Daniel

L. Block, "Will the Real Gideon Please Stand Up? Narrative Style and Intention in Judges 6–9," *Journal of the Evangelical Theological Society* 40:3 (Sept. 1997): 353–66.

[2]A. Graeme Auld, "Gideon: Hacking at the Heart of the Old Testament," *Vetus Testamentum* 39 (July 1989): 257–58. The connections Auld lists include: the call of Moses in Exodus 3:8f (6:7–9), the self-named God in Exodus 3:15 (6:10), Jacob at Peniel in Genesis 32:22–32 (8:8f), Jacob at Succoth in Genesis 33:17 (8:5f), Jacob seeing God's face in Genesis 32:24 (6:22), Samson's parents and the angel in Judges 13:3 (6:12), making of an ephod by Micah in Judges 17:5 (8:27), destroying illicit cult items in Deuteronomy 7:5 (6:25–26), Elijah and divine fire in 1 Kings 18:20–29 (6:21), Jacob's name becomes Israel in Genesis 32:28 (6:32), jewelry to make a golden calf in Exodus 32:2–4 (8:24–26), Jeroboam who built Penuel in 1 Kings 12:25 (8:8f).

[3]Tanner, "Gideon Narrative," 152.

[4]Tom Lyda, pastor of First Christian Church, Abilene, Texas, preached four sermons based on texts from the Gideon narrative as part of his D.Min. Project, "Preaching from Ancient Stories: A Collaborative Preaching Model," unpublished manuscript on file at Brite Divinity School, May 2001.

[5]An earlier version of this sermon was preached at the Brite Divinity School Kirkpatrick Summer Institute in Santa Fe, New Mexico, July 14, 2000.

[6]See *A Hebrew and English Lexicon of the Old Testament,* ed. Francis Brown, S. R. Driver, and Charles A. Briggs (Oxford: Clarendon Press, 1966), 528a.

[7]*Zohar: The Book of Enlightenment,* trans. Daniel C. Matt (New York: Paulist Press, 1983), 43.

[8]*"Let All Mortal Flesh Keep Silence,"* in Presbyterian Hymnal (Louisville: Westminster/John Knox Press, 1990), no. 5.

[9]Joseph R. Jeter, Jr., "It's Still Fun," address to Disciples ministers at the Pension Fund of the Christian Church breakfast at the General Assembly of the Christian Church (Disciples of Christ), 12 October 1999, Cincinnati, Ohio.

[10]Paddy Chayefsky, *Gideon* (New York: Carnegie Productions, Inc., 1961), 85.

[11]Ibid., 138

[12]At this point in the sermon I put on a large gold earring. If I had it to do over again, I would resist that temptation. Not having pierced ears, I had to find a clip-on. Since I did not know how to properly attach such an earring, it kept falling off. What I intended to be a mildly humorous example of distraction tumbled into hilarity, and the point was lost.

[13]Harry Emerson Fosdick, "The Power to See It Through," *Riverside Sermons* (New York: Harper & Bros., 1958), 28.

[14]Albert Outler, "Theodosius' Horse: Reflections on the Predicament of the Church Historian," *Church History* 34:3 (Sept. 1965): 251–61.

[15]Joseph R. Jeter, Jr. and Hiram J. Lester, "The Tragedy of Wickliffe Campbell," *Lexington Theological Quarterly* (July, 1987): 85–97.

[16]Alexander Campbell, cited in Jeter and Lester, 93.

[17]See J. Cheryl Exum, ed., *Virtual History and the Bible* (Leiden: Brill, 2000).

[18]Arthur John Gossip, "But When Life Tumbles In, What Then?" in *The Hero in Thy Soul* (Edinburgh: T & T Clark, 1928), 111.

[19]David Jobling, "Structuralist Criticism: The Text's World of Meaning," in *Judges and Method,* ed. Gale A. Yee (Minneapolis: Fortress Press, 1995), 101.

[20]See J. Cheryl Exum, "The Centre Cannot Hold," *Catholic Biblical Quarterly* 52 (July 1990): 416.

[21]This story strains credulity almost as much as some of the Samson stories. That 120,000 battle-hardened troops would flee before 300 men with torches and *shofars* is a tough sell, especially since torch in one hand and *shofar* in the other means no drawn sword. The text is clearly about faith, not superior military tactics.

Chapter 6: Abimelech, Disloyalty, and Retribution

[1]Naomi Steinberg, "Social Scientific Criticism: Judges 9 and Issues of Kinship," in *Judges and Method,* ed. Gale A. Yee (Minneapolis: Fortress Press, 1995), 57.

[2]Dennis T. Olson, "The Book of Judges" in *The New Interpreter's Bible,* vol. 2 (Nashville: Abingdon Press, 1998), 819.

[3]Josiah Royce, *The Philosophy of Loyalty* (New York: Macmillan, 1908), 14.

[4]Ibid., 17.

[5]Ibid., 118–19

[6]Ibid., 121.

[7]Olson, "Book of Judges," 815. The horrible slaughter of a ruling family has recently been repeated in the mountain kingdom of Nepal.

[8]Abimelech's shameful death is recalled in 2 Samuel 11:21.

[9]Volkmar Fritz, cited in T. A. Boogaart, "Stone for Stone: Retribution in the Story of Abimelech and Shechem," *Journal for the Study of the Old Testament* 32 (1985): 45.

[10]Boogaart, "Stone for Stone," 47.

[11]Barnabas Lindars, "Jotham's Fable—A New Form-Critical Analysis," *Journal of Theological Studies* 24:2 (Oct. 1973): 363.

[12]Graham S. Ogden, "Jotham's Fable: Its Structure and Function in Judges 9," *The Bible Translator* 46:3 (July 1995), 308.

[13]"MAD," *Cold War, Episode 12* (CNN: 13 Dec. 1998).

[14]See Lawrence J. Peter and Raymond Hull, *The Peter Principle* (New York: William Morrow, 1969).

[15]We note that Abimelech's sordid rule was bordered by stones. He killed his brothers on one stone and then was fatally wounded by another stone.

[16]Michael Shaara, *The Killer Angels* (New York: David McKay, 1974), 361.

Chapter 7: Jephthah and His Daughter

[1]Jephthah's birth was in some way irregular; he was probably the son of Gilead and a prostitute.

[2]Jason Bronner, "Jephtha's Daughter: A Girl Without a Dream," 1993. Used with permission.

[3]The idea that the spirit might have been responsible for the vow is repugnant and preposterous to me.

[4]For an example of such a plea set forth in midrash, see *The Book of Legends,* ed. Hayim Nahman Bialik and Yehoshua Hana Ravnitzky, trans. William G. Braude (New York: Schocken Books, 1992), 109. I am grateful to Lisa Davison for pointing this out to me.

⁵I have this information from Toni Craven.

⁶Charles Heavysege, "Jephthah's Daughter," in *Canadian Anthology,* ed. Carl F. Klinck and Reginald E. Watters (Toronto: Gage Publishing, 1974), 76. This poem is considered one of the best examples of post-romantic narratives done in Canada in the nineteenth century. I am grateful to Prof. Vernon Lindquist of Barton College for introducing me to Heavysege's work. For those, like me, who did not know what "bittern" are, they are night herons with a booming cry.

⁷Ruth Fox, "Women in the Bible and the Lectionary," *Call to Action* (June 1986): 5.

⁸Laurie Feille, conversation with author, August 2000.

⁹Scholar Lisa Davison does not see this verse in as dark a way as I do. She sees it as having a softer "thy will be done" quality. She could be right. From correspondence with the author, Aug. 14, 2001.

¹⁰One of the most vivid stories of Jephthah's birth, life, and death can be found in "Upon This Evil Earth" by Amos Oz in *Where the Jackals Howl,* trans. from the Hebrew by Nicholas de Lange and Philip Simpson (New York: Harcourt Brace Jovanovich, 1981) 168–217. Oz's story also contains an interesting description of Jephthah's daughter, giving her the name Pitdah.

¹¹Aristides and Cimon are among the best-known leaders who were ostracized and then recalled. Plutarch records a memorable story about Aristides' ostracism: "as the voters were inscribing their *ostraka,* it is said that an unlettered and utterly boorish fellow handed his *ostrakon* to Aristides, whom he took to be one of the ordinary crowd, and asked him to write *Aristides* on it. He, astonished, asked the man what possible wrong Aristides had done him. 'None whatsoever,' was the answer, 'I don't even know the fellow, but I'm tired of hearing him everywhere called The Just.' On hearing this, Aristides made no answer, but wrote his name on the *ostrakon* and handed it back." *Plutarch's Lives 2,* trans. Bernadotte Perrin (Cambridge, Mass.: Harvard Univ. Press, 1968), 233–35.

¹²David M. Gunn, "Samson of Sorrows: An Isaianic Gloss on Judges 13–16," in *Reading Between Texts: Intertextuality and the Hebrew Bible,* ed. Danna Nolan Fewell (Louisville: Westminster John Knox Press, 1992), 251.

¹³A version of this sermon previously appeared in Joseph R. Jeter, Jr., *Re/Membering* (St. Louis: Chalice Press, 1998).

¹⁴Richard Hough, *Mountbatten* (New York: Random House, 1981), and Helmut Heiber, *Goebbels,* trans. John K. Dickinson (New York: Hawthorne, 1972).

¹⁵Hough, *Mountbatten,* 80ff.

¹⁶Heiber, *Goebbels,* 215, 238.

¹⁷See Hough, *Mountbatten,* 39–40; Heiber, *Goebbels,* 356.

¹⁸Phyllis Trible, *Texts of Terror* (Philadelphia: Fortress Press, 1984), 109.

¹⁹Nikos Kazantzakis, *The Odyssey: A Modern Sequel,* trans. Kimon Friar (New York: Simon and Schuster, 1958), 233.

²⁰Trible says, "To seek the redemption of these stories [including that of Jephthah's daughter] in the resurrection is perverse. Sad stories do not have happy endings," *Texts of Terror,* 2. While she is speaking specifically of the resurrection of Jesus Christ, I suspect she would find my plea for Jephthah's daughter just as wrongheaded as I find hers.

²¹From "Lord of the Dance," words by Sydney Carter, Nineteenth-century Shaker tune adapted by Carter.

²²Nikos Kazantzakis, *The Fratricides,* trans. Athena Gianakas Dallas (New York: Simon and Schuster, 1964), 160.

²³James A. Sanders, "In the Same Night," *God Has a Story, Too* (Philadelphia: Fortress Press, 1979), 96.

²⁴The lack of a name for Jephthah's daughter has bothered people for thousands of years. It bothers me. J. Cheryl Exum suggests her namelessness is a result of her being "commemorated not for herself but as a daughter," *Tragedy and Biblical Narrative* (Cambridge: Cambridge Univ. Press, 1992), 66. Many have nevertheless felt the need to name her. Mieke Bal has written: "To name this nameless character is to violate the biblical text. Not to name her is to violate her with the text," *Death and Dissymmetry* (Chicago: Univ. of Chicago Press, 1988), 43. She has been called *Seila* in Josephus's *Biblical Antiquities* 40.1–9, cited in Cheryl Anne Brown, *No Longer Be Silent* (Louisville: Westminster John Knox Press, 1992), 100–17, and *Iphigenia* in Georg Friedrich Handel's last oratorio, *Jeptha,* 1751 (named after the daughter of Agamemnon in Greek legend, who was also sacrificed). More recently, she has been called *Bath-Jephthah,* or, more briefly, *Bath* (daughter) by Mieke Bal, 43; Exum calls her *Bat-jiftah* for its closer approximation to the Hebrew and its ease of pronunciation, "Feminist Criticism: Whose Interests Are Being Served?" in *Judges and Method,* ed. Gale A. Yee (Minneapolis: Fortress Press, 1995), 75. Lisa Davison calls her simply *Bat* in sermons she has preached on Judges 11.

²⁵Joseph R. Jeter, Jr., *Alexander Procter: The Sage of Independence* (Claremont, Calif.: Disciples Seminary Foundation, 1983), 137.

²⁶J. J. Haley, *Makers and Molders of the Reformation Movement* (St. Louis: Christian Publishing Co., 1914), 154.

²⁷The Ephraimites complained, asking Jephthah why he did not call them when he went to fight the Ammonites so they could go with him. Jephthah claimed he did call them. Out of this childish fuss, they went to war. What is even more bizarre is that this happened for a second time. The Ephraimites also complained to Gideon (8:1) that he did not call them when he went to fight against the Midianites. At least Gideon solved the problem diplomatically, instead of going to war like Jephthah, a difference that may be a demonstration of just how far Israel had slid into discord and disaster between the two leaders. One also begins to wonder why the Ephraimites always showed up after the battle was over, complaining because they did not get to fight. I think the narrator did not like Ephraimites and enjoyed ridiculing them, which may also be why the most disgusting person in Judges, the Levite of chapters 19–21, was described as an Ephraimite.

Chapter 8: Samson

¹The Samson story, as many of the stories in Judges, is laden with sexual innuendo. See J. Cheryl Exum, *Fragmented Women: Feminist (Sub)versions of Biblical Narratives* (Sheffield: JSOT Press, 1993), 61–93.

²See J. Alberto Soggin, *Judges: A Commentary,* trans. John Bowden (Philadelphia: Westminster Press, 1981), 258–59.

³H. T. Sell, *Studies of Famous Bible Women* (New York: Fleming H. Revell, 1925), 44.

⁴During the Middle Ages Samson was often seen as a prefigure of Christ. This view endures. See, e.g., Dennis T. Olson, "The Book of Judges" in *The New Interpreter's Bible,* vol. 2 (Nashville: Abingdon Press, 1998), 861–62, and

Barry Webb, "A Serious Reading of the Samson Story," *Reformed Theological Journal* 54:3 (Sept.-Dec. 1995): 120. David M. Gunn has a different twist on this idea in "Samson of Sorrows: An Isaianic Gloss on Judges 13-16," in *Reading Between Texts: Intertextuality and the Hebrew Bible*, ed. Danna Nolan Fewell (Louisville: Westminster John Knox Press, 1992), 225–53.

⁵Marvin Pope, cited in J. Cheryl Exum, "Aspects of Symmetry and Balance in the Samson Saga," *Journal for the Study of the Old Testament* 19 (1981): 7.

⁶James L. Crenshaw, *Samson* (Atlanta: John Knox Press, 1978), 151.

⁷John Milton, "Samson Agonistes," cited in Webb, "A Serious Reading," 116.

⁸Webb, "A Serious Reading," 116–17.

⁹Ibid., 110, 112.

¹⁰Olson, "Book of Judges," 854.

¹¹Douglas Todd, "Shrinking Heroes," *Fort Worth Star-Telegram*, 31 March 2001, 3G.

¹²J. Cheryl Exum, "Lovis Corinth's *Blinded Samson,"* *Biblical Interpretation* 6:3–4 (1998): 412.

¹³Although Samson dies, Israel is "delivered," so to speak, and Samson is reintegrated into society through his deliverance and his burial in the familial tomb.

¹⁴J. Cheryl Exum and J. William Whedbee, "Isaac, Samson and Saul: Reflections on the Comic and Tragic Visions," *Semeia* 32 (1985): 8–9.

¹⁵Exum, "Lovis Corinth's *Blinded Samson*," 415. Corinth's painting is here reproduced with the permission of the National Gallery, Berlin, Germany.

¹⁶Ibid., 424.

¹⁷Ron O'Grady, "Strength in Weakness," in *Preaching through the Apocalypse*, ed. Cornish R. Rogers and Joseph Jeter (St. Louis, Chalice Press, 1992), 85.

¹⁸John W. Vannorsdall, "Samson," *Weavings* 8 (Sept.–Oct. 1993): 37–40. The following paragraph is adapted from Vannorsdall's article.

¹⁹Ibid., 40.

²⁰Ibid.

²¹Jimmy Buffett, "Margaritaville," in *Changes of Latitude, Changes of Attitude* (ABC Records, 1977).

²²See Crenshaw, *Samson*, 140.

²³This is also a little strange, in that nine verses earlier, we read that "the LORD used to speak to Moses face to face, as one speaks to a friend" (33:11).

²⁴Manoah's wife remains one of those interesting unnamed women of the Bible. J. Clinton McCann, building on a suggestion by Adele Reinhartz, suggests that "the mutual namelessness stresses the intimacy between the angel and Samson's mother." He goes on to say that "Samson's mother is the real hero of the Samson story...that of all the characters in Judges 13–16, an unnamed woman bears the closest relationship to God and models the behavior that God wills for God's people," *Judges*, Interpretation: A Bible Commentary for Preaching and Teaching (Louisville: Westminster John Knox Press, 2003), 149.

²⁵Richard G. Bowman, "Narrative Criticism: Human Purpose in Conflict with Divine Presence," in *Judges and Method*, ed. Gale A. Yee (Minneapolis: Fortress Press, 1995), 39.

²⁶Fred B. Craddock, *Preaching* (Nashville: Abingdon Press, 1985), 30.

[27]The previous two paragraphs have been adapted from my unpublished sermon "In the Middle of the Blessing."

[28]I am grateful to J. Cheryl Exum for pointing out this to me.

[29]Zora Neale Hurston, *Their Eyes Were Watching God* (Philadelphia: J. B. Lippincott, 1937), 191.

[30]Sheldon B. Kopp, *If You Meet the Buddha on the Road, Kill Him!* (Ben Lomond, Calif.: Science and Behavior Books, 1972), 158.

[31]Hayim Nahman Bialik and Yehoshua Hana Ravnitzky, *The Book of Legends* (New York: Schocken Books, 1992), 110.

[32]Jon Berquist, *Reclaiming Her Story: The Witness of the Women in the Old Testament* (St. Louis: Chalice Press, 1992), 95.

[33]I have warned against interpreting Samson by using modern psychological categories. Terrorism, however, is quite ancient and, technology aside, operates in basically the same way it did thousands of years ago.

[34]For a sermon on these two roads, see Joseph R. Jeter, Jr., "Two Roads to Peace: Lessons from the Joseph Saga," *Impact* 15 (1985): 21–27.

[35]The text does not say whether Delilah was a Philistine. But there is no doubt that she was in their employ.

[36]Susan Ackerman suggests that Samson was so bumbling in his role as an Israelite hero that it seems almost as if his story was written by a Philistine whose intention was to poke fun at Samson. See Ackerman, "What If Judges Had Been Written by a Philistine?" in *Virtual History and the Bible,* ed. J. Cheryl Exum (Leiden: Brill, 2000), 33.

[37]For more on this idea, see Athalya Brenner and Fokkelien van Dijk-Hemmes, *On Gendering Texts: Female and Male Voices in the Hebrew Bible* (Leiden: Brill, 1993).

[38]Mary Cartledge-Hayes, *To Love Delilah: Claiming the Women of the Bible* (San Diego: LuraMedia, 1990), 43.

[39]Alice Ogden Bellis, *Helpmates, Harlots, and Heroes: Women's Stories in the Hebrew Bible* (Louisville: Westminster John Knox Press, 1994), 126.

[40]See Joseph R. Jeter, Jr., "Ruth People in an Esther World," *Patterns of Preaching,* ed. Ronald J. Allen (St. Louis: Chalice Press, 1998), 49–56.

[41]Claudia V. Camp, *Wise, Strange and Holy: The Strange Woman in the Making of the Bible* (Sheffield: Sheffield Academic Press, 2000), 122.

[42]Tammi J. Schneider, *Judges,* Berit Olam: Studies in Hebrew Narrative and Poetry (Collegeville, Minn.: Liturgical Press, 2000), 224.

Chapter 9: Micah and the Danites

[1]See the excursus on Micah's dilemma in Joseph R. Jeter, Jr., *Crisis Preaching* (Nashville: Abingdon Press, 1998), 53–58.

[2]Tammi J. Schneider, *Judges,* Berit Olam: Studies in Hebrew Narrative and Poetry(Collegeville, Minn.: Liturgical Press, 2000), 229. Some believe 17–21 is more logically attached to that which follows–1 Samuel.

[3]See, e.g., Robert H. O'Connell, *The Rhetoric of the Book of Judges* (Leiden: Brill, 1996), 231f. The same can be said of 19–21 and 1:1–2:5, but they are not my concern here.

[4]Schneider, *Judges,* 229.

[5]Philip E. Satterthwaite, "'No King in Israel': Narrative Criticism and Judges 17–21," *Tyndale Bulletin* 44:1 (May 1993): 77–79.

⁶Ibid.

⁷Michael K. Wilson, "'As You Like It': The Idolatry of Micah and the Danites (Judges 17–18)," *Reformed Theological Review* 54:2 (May-August 1995): 74–76, 81.

⁸Schneider, *Judges,* 230–31. Remember that Gideon also had two names.

⁹Gale A. Yee, "Ideological Criticism: Judges 17–21 and the Dismembered Body," in *Judges and Method* (Minneapolis: Fortress Press, 1995), 158.

¹⁰Dale R. Davis, "Comic Literature–Tragic Theology: A Study of Judges 17–18," *Westminster Theological Journal* 46 (1984): 158.

¹¹Phillip McMillion, "Worship in Judges 17–18," in *Worship and the Hebrew Bible,* ed. N. Patrick Graham, Rick R. Mars, and Steven L. McKenzie, Journal for the Study of the Old Testament, Supplement 284(Sheffield: Sheffield Academic Press, 1999), 238–39. See also Dennis T. Olson, "The Book of Judges" in *The New Interpreter's Bible,* vol. 2 (Nashville: Abingdon Press, 1998), 870–71.

¹²McMillion, "Worship," 241.

¹³Yairah Amit, "Hidden polemic in the conquest of Dan: Judges xvii-xviii," *Vetus Testamentum* 40:1 (January 1990): 19.

¹⁴McMillion, "Worship," 228.

¹⁵Yee, "Ideological Criticism," 158. Her position has been criticized in Andrew H. Mayes, "Deuteronomistic Royal Ideology in Judges 17–21," *Biblical Interpretation* 9:3 (2001): 241–58.

¹⁶John Hercus, *God Is God* (London: Hodder & Stoughton, 1971), 186.

¹⁷Excerpted from Joseph R. Jeter, Jr., "It's Still Fun," Address to Disciples ministers at the Pension Fund of the Christian Church breakfast at the General Assembly of the Christian Church (Disciples of Christ), 12 October 1999, Cincinnati, Ohio.

¹⁸John Milton, "Lycidas," in *The Literature of England,* vol. 1 (Chicago: Scott, Foresman & Co., 1958), 712.

¹⁹This is, of course, representative of the Judahite position, which does not like rival places of worship. While I could not support a contemporary analogy suggesting that only large worship centers are legitimate, neither could I support churches or temples acquired by violence.

Chapter 10: The Levite's Wife—Not Every Story Has a Happy Ending

¹See Tony Campolo, *It's Friday, But Sunday's Coming* (Waco, Tx.: Word, 1982).

²Eugene Boring, "Everything Is Going to Be All Right," *Preaching through the Apocalypse,* ed. Cornish R. Rogers and Joseph R. Jeter, Jr. (St. Louis: Chalice Press, 1992), 75–82.

³The first line of *Brian's Song,* a TV movie about football player Brian Piccolo.

⁴William Shakespeare, *King Richard II,* act 1, scene 1, line 188.

⁵Stephen Spender, "I Think Continually of Those Who Were Truly Great," in *Collected Poems 1928–1985* (New York: Random House, 1986), 30.

⁶"U.N. Cites Honor Killings Rise," Associated Press, April 7, 2000.

⁷Riffat Hassan, Professor of Religious Studies at the University of Louisville, interviewed on "A Matter of Honor," *Nightline,* ABC News Transcript 4624 (16 February 1999), 5.

[8]"A Matter of Honor," *Nightline*, ABC News Transcript 4623 (15 February 1999), 4.

[9]The NRSV says that she returned home because she was angry with the Levite. The verb *zanah* can mean that she "fornicated" or "played the harlot" against her husband, but Gail Yee reminds us that the act of leaving her husband could be understood within the patriarchal culture as metaphoric fornication, "Ideological Criticism: Judges 17–21 and the Dismembered Body," *Judges and Method* (Minneapolis: Fortress Press, 1995), 162. And Mieke Bal suggests that we may be dealing with a form of "older marriage," called *patrilocal,* in which the wife stays at her father's house, *Death and Dissymmetry,* (Chicago: Univ. of Chicago Press, 1988), 84–85. Frankly, I can think of no reason in her culture for a woman to do what the Levite's wife did other than the severest of abuse. I recently saw a play called "Judges 19." In discussions afterward with the author and star of the play, Ruth Margraff, she told me that the idea for the play was born in her own childhood experience. Her father, a traveling Baptist preacher, preached for a whole year all over Ohio on Judges 19. His point was that if the "concubine" had only stayed where she belonged, with the Levite, none of the ensuing tragedy would have occurred. Application: if women would only stay home where they belong, much of the world's problems would not occur. I think this text has nothing to do with stay-at-home moms and everything to do with spousal abuse. Blaming women for leaving an abusive situation still occurs, and it saddens me to see people ground in this text their demand that women stay put in such situations.

[10]How different is this callous demand from the gentle insistence of Jesus in Mark 5: "Talitha, cum"!

[11]This scene is based on a comment by Toni Craven, 12 April 2000.

[12]Robertson Davies, *Murther and Walking Spirits* (New York: Viking, 1991), 203–4.

[13]Tony Evans, "Spiritual Purity," in *Seven Promises of a Promise Keeper,* ed. Al Janssen and Larry K. Weedens (Colorado Springs: Focus on the Family Publishing, 1994), 79–80, cited by Tracy Dunn-Noland, "Promise Keepers or Patriarchal Kings," *Brite Student Journal* 2 (Spring 1996): 21. Italics in quotation are original.

[14]Jerome Socolovsky, "War Crimes Panel Examines Sex Case," Associated Press, March 19, 2000.

[15]I am also hopeful that positive stories of biblical women, such as *The Red Tent* by Anita Diamant (New York: Picador USA, 1997), might open new possibilities for dialogue and understanding.

[16]David Buttrick, *Preaching Jesus Christ* (Philadelphia: Fortress Press, 1988), 30.

[17]The eulogy was published in *Unity* (May-June 1984). It may also be found in Amiri Baraka, *Eulogies* (New York: Marsilio, 1996), 48–54. I used this quotation earlier in *Crisis Preaching* (Nashville: Abingdon Press, 1998), 80. I am also aware that Baraka's name is very similar to that of one of the major dramatis personae in Judges.

[18]See Claudia V. Camp, *Wise, Strange and Holy: The Strange Woman in the Making of the Bible* (Sheffield: Sheffield Academic Press, 2000), 120.

[19]Tammi J. Schneider, *Judges,* Berit Olam: Studies in Hebrew Narrative and Poetry (Collegeville, Minn.: Liturgical Press, 2000), 289.

[20]See Roina Tifiga Fa'atauva'a, "A Critical Study of the Status of Women in Samoa," unpub. ms., Pacific Theological College, Suva, Fiji, September 1991.

[21]The Hip-Hop Music Award went to Eminem for "The Marshall Mathers LP." See Steve Blow, "Nothing Lyrical about Smut and Hate," *Dallas Morning News*, 27 August 2000, A33.

Conclusion

[1]J. Clinton McCann, *Judges*, Interpretation (Louisville: Westminster John Knox Press, 2003), 2.

[2]A useful monograph on the use of analogy in preaching is that of Stephen Farris, *Preaching That Matters* (Louisville: Westminster John Knox, 1998).